THE LIFE & WORK OF
Mary Brodrick

SARAH R. ENTERLINE, M.A.

FOREWORD BY
TED W. WRIGHT

THE LIFE & WORK OF
Mary Brodrick

SARAH R. ENTERLINE, M.A.

FOREWORD BY
TED W. WRIGHT

Some included images are taken from public domain publications in the 1800's.

Cover photo courtesy of Peggy Joy Egyptology Library

Enterline Press
www.enterlinepress.com

Cover/Interior Design by Matt Enterline

First Printing: October 2023

ISBN 979-8-9879332-2-0

Dedication

To Dr. Joseph Holden ~

*For being like Mary's mentors and
encouraging my gifts despite my gender.*

Table of Contents

Foreword

Two pivotal events in the eighteenth and nineteenth centuries opened a portal into the world of ancient Egypt: the discovery of the Rosetta Stone in 1799, and its eventual deciphering by the French scholar, Jean-François Champollion in 1822. With a knowledge of how to properly translate hieroglyphics, scholars both in Europe and America were now poised to gain a fuller and more nuanced understanding of ancient Egypt than ever before. In the nineteenth century, archaeology was little more than glorified grave robbing fueled by an intense nationalistic rivalry between England and France. A little over fifty years after Champollion's translation of hieroglyphics, when Egyptology was still in its infancy, a French university student named Gaston Maspero showed a great proclivity for ancient languages, including Sanskrit and hieroglyphics. He promised to be one of the leading Egyptologists of his day, and by the end of the 1870's was considered to be the greatest Egyptologist in France. In 1880, under sponsorship of the French government, Maspero would travel to Egypt to begin an archaeological mission which would eventually become the Institut Français d'Archéologie Orientale (French Institute for Oriental Archaeology) in Cairo.

When Maspero taught Egyptology at the Collège de France, a young English woman named Mary Brodrick sought to study under him. Maspero, along with fellow scholar Ernst Renan, strongly objected to her attending. When Brodrick insisted, Maspero further appealed to the Sorbonne who found that a woman studying Egyptology at the college violated none of its rules. After eventually gaining his respect, Broderick traveled to Greece and Egypt with Maspero in the 1890's, working under his direction. She became one of the first female archaeologists to excavate in Egypt. In 1888, Brodrick went on study at University College London under Stuart Poole who co-founded the Egypt Exploration Society (Fund) along with another notable early female Egyptologist of the day named

Amelia Edwards. Because of Brodrick's knowledge of Egyptian history and antiquities, she lectured at the prestigious British Museum, where she also studied Egyptology under Sir William Matthews Flinders Petrie. Petrie held the first chair of Egyptology in England, and is considered by many historians to be the father of scientific, biblical archaeology.[1] To say that Mary Brodrick was a pioneer is an understatement, yet she is hardly known by the wider public today.

Along with Gertrude Bell (1868-1926), who founded the Iraq Museum in Bagdad in 1926, and Amelia Edwards, whose travel account, *A Thousand Miles Up the Nile* (1877), brought an increased awareness to protect ancient Egyptian monuments, Mary Brodrick deserves to be known and read by a wider audience today— especially Christians. Along with these other notable women, Brodrick was ahead of her time. In addition to her remarkable experience in the field and in the classroom, Brodrick utilized her vast knowledge of history and archaeology in the service of her Christian faith.

History and Archaeology in the Service of Christian Faith

In 1908, Brodrick published a book titled, *The Trial and Crucifixion of Jesus* by the notable publisher, John Murray, in London. The book was based on live lectures she gave throughout the United Kingdom years before. In her book, Brodrick references ancient sources such as Cicero, Tacitus, Suetonius, Josephus, as well as her former professor Ernst Renan, from the Collège de France. She also consulted discoveries in Israel by the Palestine Exploration Fund (known as the PEF)— a society dedicated to topographical surveys and ethnography in Ottoman, Israel. Archaeology was a burgeoning science in the early twentieth century, yet Brodrick had the foresight to apply the latest historical and scholarly research to Christ's trial and crucifixion as it is recorded in the four Gospels.

....

1   See, P.R.S. Moorey, *A Century of Biblical Archaeology* (Louisville, KY: Westminster/ John Knox Press), 26-53.

She saw archaeology's relevance for illuminating and affirming the historicity of the New Testament.

Archaeology has come quite a long way since Brodrick's *Trial*. Since that time, her trust in the historical reliability of the Gospels has been confirmed a hundred times over. Since 1908, New Testament critics have continued to publish books espousing a skeptical view of the historical reliability of the biblical text. A host of discoveries in the past few years, however, has tempered those skeptical objections.

- In 1997, Israeli archaeologist Ehud Netzer discovered the mausoleum and stone coffin of King Herod the Great (Luke 2) at Herodium. Archaeologist Dr. Jodi Magness of UNC Chapel Hill hailed Netzer's discovery as one of the greatest discoveries in Israel since the Dead Sea Scrolls.[2]

- In 1990, the ossuary and likely bones of Caiaphas, the High Priest who presided over the trial of Christ (Matt. 26:57-68), were discovered in Jerusalem. Caiaphas is mentioned by name in the New Testament, as well as in the writings of first century historian, Flavius Josephus. The name inscribed on the ossuary is the exact name recorded in Josephus.

- In 1961, as Italian archaeologists were excavating near a Roman amphitheater at the ancient seaport of Caesarea Maritima, they discovered a dedicatory inscription dating to the time of the Roman emperor Tiberius. The Latin inscription mentions by name and title, "Pontius Pilate, prefect of Judea." Then, during the 1968-69 excavations at Herodium, under the direction of Gideon Foerster, a copper alloy ring was discovered along with hundreds of other objects. In 2018, the ring was taken to the laboratory for a thorough cleaning and scholarly examination. Inscribed on the ring, in partly damaged Greek, was the name "Pilates," along with an engraved amphora in the middle. The ring very likely belonged to Pontius Pilate.

....

2   Jodi Magness, "Herod the Great's Self-Representation Through His Tomb at Herodium," In *Journal of Ancient Judaism* Volume 10, issue 3, December 2019, 258-287.

Like Mary Brodrick before her, Sarah Enterline is also a pioneer who has been breaking new ground in the subject of historical apologetics for several years. We are greatly in her debt for her excavation of the life and work of Susanna Newcome (1728) who was one of the first women in history to publish a book on, and publicly engage in, the discipline of Christian Apologetics. Now Sarah has brought to the surface the life and work of Egyptologist and archaeologist, Mary Brodrick. *Digging Deeper* will be of great interest for those who want to know more about the fascinating history of archaeology and Egyptology, and also for those who wish to continue in her footsteps to *contend earnestly for the faith which once and for all delivered to the saints* (Jude 1:3).

Ted W. Wright

Executive Director of Epic Archaeology
Chicago, IL
Lent 2023

Editor's Introduction:

Growing up, some of my favorite movies were *Indiana Jones: Raiders of Lost Ark*, and *Indiana Jones and the Last Crusade.* I was extremely interested in how the Bible and History were related to each other, given the conflicting narratives I heard being a Christian that attended both public and Sunday school my whole life. It seemed so exciting to be the one to find something from biblical history like the Ark of the Covenant. If an object that featured in so many biblical stories could be found, it would help so many be confident in their faith that the Bible can be trusted as truth. The more and more I learned about apologetics, biblical archaeology, and manuscript evidence, the more I thought about being an archaeologist. I majored in history and Bible in college, and volunteered at the local museum just to get experience handling and cataloging artifacts. When my son came along, I realized being an archaeologist in the field for months at a time was not going to be a viable career option for me. That's when my career shifted to teaching history and Bible instead. However, I still love watching movies and documentaries about archaeology, and Egyptology has especially fascinated me. I mean, who didn't want to be the characters of Rick or Evelyn when the *Mummy* movies first came out? (Minus the presence of a lifeforce-sucking mummy monster, of course.)

As my academic career and research continued, I began to focus on women in history, specifically their contribution to Christianity and the Church as a whole. That's when I discovered Mary Brodrick, who I was instantly envious of! This woman, who lived at the turn of the 20th century, was an archaeologist traveling around Egypt when Howard Carter discovered the untouched tomb of Tut-ankh-amen! I appreciate her as well because in her work, she described the things she saw so vividly, you feel as though you were there yourself. It was recorded that when she spoke about Egypt, "her audiences were wafted away from all present surroundings into the ages of the past. The whole expression of her face changed as though she were actually there, in the warm dry air, the glowing, glittering sand with the indescribable sunsets, and the roll up of the deep blue mantle of night... People, places, things rose again as [Brodrick] described them with punctilious accuracy, clearness, humor, and insight into character." [1]

After Mary Brodrick passed away, her friend and executor Eversley Chaning Robinson, the wife of Sir Arnold Percy Robinson, collected and edited her unpublished works in a book entitled, *Egypt: Papers and Lectures by the late Mary Brodrick*. The Introduction of that work included an extensive biography of Mary's life that makes up the second chunk of *Part One* of this book. The first source that gives insight to Mary's life is the *Memoir* published after she died in 1933. Much of it is sourced from her own writings and remembrances, and clearly details the awe and reverence Mary had for God. The purpose of the **bold type** in *Part One* is to call attention to details that I found most impressive about her. It was said that she was so full of God's light you could see it on her face. May we follow Mary's example in reflecting God so fully that His light pours out of all of us the way it did her.

Part Two is a blended Scriptural sequence of events by myself, and confirmed by Brodrick in her text. These events include Jesus' arrest, trials, condemnation, crucifixion, and burial. Often when we read the Gospels individually, while each valuable in their own right, we lose some details that, when reading for devotional purposes, is not that big of a deal. However, when we are reading to understand the peculiarities of Jewish trial law and an accurate timeline of events, it is important to have all the details in front of us at the same time. It is also important as Brodrick's Lectures go along this sequence and take all four Gospels into account.

Part Three is the 1908 work by Mary Brodrick, *The Trial and Crucifixion of Jesus Christ of Nazareth*, edited for a modern audience. It includes her original Preface, Lecture 1: The Arrest, Lecture 2:

....

1   Egypt papers, xii

The Trial and Condemnation, and Lecture 3: The Crucifixion and the Site of the Holy Tomb. I have tried to leave as much of Mary's voice as possible, and only edited a few things for ease of reading, such as clarifying the outline of her arguments and adjusting the King James Version to various modern versions of the Bible, like the NKJV, ESV, NIV, or HCSB. I determined which modern version to use based on which one communicated the text most accurately. Lastly, I call attention to items of apologetic interest in *Part Three* by putting them in **bold text.**

I pray that Mary's deep dive into the details of the last day of our Savior's life blesses you as much as it has blessed me.

In His Service,

Sarah R. Enterline

Part One

The Life of Mary Brodrick
1858-1933

Portrait from: Janssen, Rosaling & Jac. (1999) "Excavating in the Petrie Museum"
in A. Leahy & J. Tait (Eds.) Studies on Ancient Egypt in Honour of H.S. Smith.
London: Egypt Exploration Society, pp. 151-156.

Artist is probably Norah Fulcher.

Biography

Mary Brodrick, "May" to her friends, was born in Hackney, London on 05 April 1858, to Mary (née Smith Haviside) and Thomas Brodrick. She was baptized a month later, on 08 May 1858.[1] She spent her childhood in Salisbury (Wiltshire Co.) and London, where her father was a lawyer. A census from 1861 shows Mary and her sisters, Edith and Ethel, lived with their parents in Liberty of the Close, St. Martin, Salisbury.[2] Her parents later had a boy they named Cecil. There is not much more information on her childhood, but it appears as a girl, she was given a French History of Egypt which sparked a lifelong passion for the study of Egyptology.

Brodrick was not only a prolific archaeologist and Egyptologist, she was also a devout Christian and an active member of the Society of Biblical Archaeology. Her training in the archaeology of the Near East and Roman law made her an expert on Biblical history as well. She delivered a series of lectures that were later published in 1908 under the title, *The Trial and Crucifixion of Jesus Christ of Nazareth*. The arguments of her book deem it an excellent work of Christian apologetics, as Brodrick logically and expertly answers the challenges to the crucifixion and resurrection of Jesus Christ that were (and still are to this day) commonly proposed by skeptics.

Unfortunately, not much can be found regarding the reception and influence of Mary Brodrick's *Trial*. The *Book Review Digest* had one short review regarding it: "The three lectures, short though they are, are interesting in every detail, and deserve the attention

---

1   Record Url: https://www.ancestry.co.uk/imageviewer/collections/1558/images/31280_195156-00385
Source Citation: London Metropolitan Archives; London, England; Reference Number: p79/jn1/037
2   Record Url: https://www.ancestry.co.uk/imageviewer/collections/8767/images/WILRG9_1311_1315-0968
  Source Citation: Class: RG9; Piece: 1315; Folio: 56; Page: 16; GSU roll: 542794

of the ordinary reader as well as the New Testament student and scholar. Miss Brodrick has certainly studied Jewish law to good purpose." – Ath. 1908, 1:666. May 30.[3]

In 1924, she established the Mary Brodrick Prize in Geography at University College, gave a generous donation toward the new College Hall building in 1929, and ultimately bequeathed her entire archaeological library of books to College Hall. After spending her retirement in Villa Primavera Bordighera, Italy, and never having married, Mary died at Stoneycrest Hindhead Surrey, England on 13 July 1933. Her effects were left to her brother, Cecil Brodrick, and her friend, Eversley Chaning Robinson.[4]

Transcription of the Memoir of
Dr. Mary Brodrick, Ph. D., F.R.G.S.
Dame of Grace of St. John of Jerusalem
(Traveler, Writer, Lecturer, Scholar)[5]

Miss Brodrick left the following description of herself, written shortly before she died.

It is not possible to bring her more forcibly before us than by printing this as an introduction to this little Memoir:

Foreword

"I am a Back Number, and an old one at that—a gregarious wanderer and lover of [humans] and things. The greater part of my life has been spent in foreign lands—Europe and the Near East. I am not an official of any sort or kind, either government or commercial, merely a wanderer on whom Heaven, Fate, or my

....

3   *The Book Review Digest, 1908*. Minneapolis: The H.W. Wilson Company, 1908, p. 46.
4   Record Url: https://www.ancestry.co.uk/imageviewer/collections/1904/ images/31874_223141- 00474
Source Information: Ancestry.com. *England & Wales, National Probate Calendar (Index of Wills and*
Administrations), 1858-1995 [database on-line]. Provo, UT, USA: Ancestry.com Operations, Inc., 2010.
5   December 1933, Printed by Giuseppe Bessone, in Bordighera, Italy.

Forebears bestowed the blessed gift of picking up colloquially many strange tongues and using them quite ungrammatically but sufficiently as a means of communication. I have no pretensions to be literary, scientific, or political—merely inquisitive—and as this lucky aptitude for understanding people and tongues gave me an insight into the minds of humans, I was sometimes able to give information not altogether useless to the 'Powers that be.'"

Memoir[6]

Ageless in spirit, gracious and inspiring in personality, Miss Brodrick made of her life a treasured memory to those who knew her.

Profound humility walked hand in hand with her genius. Unremitting work to find the truth and give it to the world was the essence of her life. "Measure thy life not by the wine drunk, but by the wine poured out" was the spirit in which she lived. Generosity, fearlessness, and a joyous love of righteous battle were the assets of her character.

"Battle is the spice of life" is perhaps the one saying of Miss Brodrick's which brings her most vividly before us. To her it was glory, and with a splendid fund of humor, knowledge, and tender sympathy, she battled royally and fearlessly all her life. Being peculiarly sensitive in mind and body, life as a battle was inevitable for her from infancy. *Joie de vivre*, fun, determination, and the intellectual atmosphere of her home, carried her through these early struggles, though not without leaving honorable scars—and a distressing sense of loneliness was often with her.

Had she found the particular sympathy and support her genius needed, doubtless she would have become a pioneer in her work, which her ardent nature always hoped to do—But then her walk in life might have been in a smaller and more rarified sphere, and the power of her inspiration and genius less wide in its circle of light.

....

6   No author named, just a note that says, "A small tribute by one who knew Her. No one will ever get her 'All'."

In her very young womanhood, she did receive this special understanding and sympathy for a short time [by an unnamed friend]: only to be wrenched from her by [the untimely death of that very same person]. Out of the complexes of infancy, childhood, youth, and young womanhood our beloved friend fought her way triumphantly— She rose above them, trod them under her, and few ever suspected [she had faced them at all].

Miss Brodrick was a member of a very large family. Her parents were interested in intellectual pursuits, more especially perhaps in art and music, and they entertained some of the most interesting people of the day.

On one particular day, George Eliot and Mr. Lewis came to stay. Miss Brodrick and her beautiful sister were sent for the next morning to be introduced to these great people. George Eliot made some admiring remark about the sister, then turning to Miss Brodrick, drew her up to her knee, and putting her hand across her forehead said very earnestly in a curiously deep voice: "God Almighty never made this child with this shaped head for nothing. She will do something someday." The deep-set kindly eyes and the low voice with its curious timbre made an impression on that child which was never forgotten. It was planting the first idea that one could perhaps somewhen or somehow do something.

This then was the spark which kindled the young mind and sent her forward to work, to laugh, and to sympathize, **touching the stream of human beings that she passed with the inspiration of her gallant personality.**

The home was in the Close at Salisbury, so near the old Cathedral, that through the open windows the organ could be heard and even at times the singing. In these surroundings Miss Brodrick absorbed deeply the beauty of the old Close and Cathedral, and the atmosphere of learning, dignity, and reverence that surrounded her.

Music she loved, and she had both capacity for singing and playing. The music at the Cathedral was a special delight to her, and even the names as well as the anthems she heard there were remembered all her life. She watched eagerly the new organ being erected, nothing escaped her—sixty years later she described it in detail, as though she had seen it the day before.

Miss Brodrick's interest in Egyptian archaeology started when, as a girl, she was given a French History of Egypt. This lit up the direction her work was to take. From then onwards instead of refusing to learn history as she had done hitherto, she absorbed it from every source, Egypt being the center from which all other studies radiated.

When the light of that [aforementioned] perfect and inspiring friendship came into her life, all this interest was further stimulated, and as it slowly passed away from her, she was left with this bidding. "Do not waste your life grieving, go forward with your Egyptian interests. My soul is the sword, my body is the sheath, God draws the sword for his own use." Such were the thoughts left with her. A little black figure, shaken to the foundations, utterly alone, yet always faithful to this memory, set forth into the world to work, to learn, and to fight for herself and others, and to justify the love that had come, and had been taken from her.

Miss Brodrick went first to the Sorbonne and after some difficulty in being admitted as the first woman student, she settled down to appreciate to the full the lectures of her great Professors Maspero and Renan. Later Dr. Stuart Poole and Mr. Le Page Renouf of the British Museum took interest in, and helped forward the eager clever student. The University of London and College Hall opened their doors to her and in so doing, admitted one who never forgot to return in full measure all that was possible, in gratitude for the learning help and encouragement she received from them.

From being **the first woman lecturer in the British Museum** she went to many places in England, Scotland, Egypt and the Riviera, to give lectures with ever increasing success, till **she became acknowledged by many as the finest lecturer of her time.**

Besides this work, she coached medical students in Materia

Medica, gave music lessons, acted as Secretary to the Principal of College Hall, and wrote articles for many papers. Then came the busy years of her archaeological work in Egypt. Her dahabîyeh[7] with its twenty-three men whom she had to [captain], and her vivid life of intense interest, added to which was the association with people of historic note.

About this same period she was given the honor of being entrusted with the revision of *Murray's Guides to Palestine, Syria,* and *the Lebanon*, and the rewriting of the *Guide to Egypt*. In those days Murray's Guides attained a very high standard of scholarship and knowledge and this was no mean honor, coveted by many.

The translation of Mariette Bey's *Aperçu de l'histoire d'Egypt* and the editing of Brugsch Bey's *Egypt under the Pharaohs*, followed by her own writings of *The Dictionary of Egyptian Archaeology* and *The Trial and Crucifixion of Jesus Christ of Nazareth*, all show to what wide scholarship and learning Miss Brodrick attained.

[She had attained such a status that people were lining up to accompany her on her many trips through Egypt. An ad to accompany her and one of her co-authors reads as follows:

"A Winter on the Nile in a Dahabîyeh. Miss Brodrick, Ph. D. and Miss Anderson Morton wish to arrange for a small party to accompany them up the Nile during the ensuing winter. Special facilities are offered to those desiring to study the Archaeology of Ancient Egypt; and ample time will be given for seeing thoroughly, and without unnecessary fatigue, all places and objects of interest. For full particulars apply to Miss Brodrick, London."][8]

With all this close brain work, needing the utmost application and accuracy, Miss Brodrick never became a "blue stocking"[9] or lost her sense of fun and gaiety.

....

7   A luxury sailing boat for cruising down the Nile.
8   John Murray "Correspondence with Mary Brodrick" Collection, National Library of Scotland, rec. July 22, 2022.
9   An overly intellectual or literary woman, often used in the past as a derogative term.

The mind and spirit so delicately sensitive, so eager to know and search out the Truth, registered every beautiful sight, sound, and thought. Ugly evil impressions had no place. Incapable of absorbing them, she spat them from her in what she amusingly described as "spit cat rages", and she refused in disgust, to read the many horrible books of [the] day. **This extreme purity of mind and crystal spirit reflected itself in her face, her person, her habits, and her home. All were spotless and in order.**

There was no deception, no seeing round corners, no exaggeration, or muddy uncertainties of right or wrong—but always a straight march forward wherever she chose to go. Miss Brodrick's last home, her study, her books, the quotations she loved, the people she admired, her writings, her tastes, her habits, and above all her work, show one point towards which everything converged— and that was the desire to find the Divine Truth.

With her this longing was perhaps more conscious and intense than with many, the search more strenuous revealing itself in everything she did. Night and day it was with her. **The one book from which she was never parted was her Greek Testament and she read and pondered over it not as a duty, but because she loved it, every early morning of her life till very near the end. She listened with every side of her many-sided nature to catch "that still small voice", and the cry "Oh, that I might find Him" was the impelling impetus which drove her to search out the heart and beauty of all she saw, read, or heard.**

Reverence was innate in her and strongly so. It shone through the words she spoke, the tone of her voice, the look on her face. She knew quickly when she was treading on holy ground and walked softly. All great things produced by God or man were holy in her sight, and instinctively there was a hush in her heart as she drew near. She searched for Light and it transfigured her. "She was like the sun shining", but she knew it not.

The striking appearance, the brilliant smile, the look of wisdom, learning, and integrity on her face, drew most great minds to her. Yet she could play with the most frivolous and "flatten her nose against shop windows with the best" as she would say. **Nothing was too much trouble for her to search out—she took as much joy and interest to explain to one as she did to four or five hundred at a lecture.**

The long hours of labor she put into her lectures and addresses were amazing, in one so full of genius—but only her very best satisfied her—all she gave was given with her whole soul. With such armor she fought the battle of life and it was a hard and long one which she sustained undaunted to the end.

It was this experience that led her, in what proved to be her farewell to her College in 1932, to say in her address that **"Life is one long battle which one and all must wage in some form or other, often desperate but also a joy, even though we are [sometimes forced] to fight better and perhaps with changed weapons tomorrow."** In spite of her last illness and pain, she insisted upon the terrible journey to England to battle again when sufficiently recovered.

When at last she felt she was slipping away she said, "I should like to live if I can be of use to anyone, but not if only a nuisance", and later "I can't fight any more".

A great storm of wind and rain raged round the house, rattled the windows and the doors and moaned in the chimney.

"And out of the storm came a still small voice". Then a great peace and transcendent beauty.

"So He giveth His Beloved sleep". **A noble life, nobly fought.**

"The spirit and glow of her work, will remain with us, for she had the genius that does not perish and the spark of life that does not pass away".

Transcription of Mary's Biography from *Egypt: Papers*[10]

Many of May Brodrick's friends have asked for her biography. She found her inspiration in the land of Egypt and gave the best years of her life to research, lectures, and writing on that subject. The genius of her rare personality shines through this work. It is therefore decided to edit and publish some of her lectures, and by kind permission of the Editors to republish some of the articles written by her for the *Scotsman, Egyptian Gazette, Guardian*, etc.

When May Brodrick first visited Egypt, probably in 1888, after a warning against spending the winter in England [due to her health], she joined some friends and the man of the party, being in the Irrigation Department, took her up the Nile when he went on inspection. Nothing escaped her keen observation. Once having seen the country, its scientific problems, its mystery, its grandeur, its art, its history, its fascinations were irresistible, whirling her into the vortex of research, and [into] work with other minds.

Her experiences in the course of attaining adequate preparation for Egyptological work are given from her own dictation:
"As University College could not at that time provide a thorough training in archaeology and Egyptology, I went to the Sorbonne and the Collège de France. I saw Maspero[11], the linguist, the historian, the archaeologist, the master—but not the artist—a wonderful lecturer. He would sit down in the armchair, this fat little thing, then in the quietest, most ordinary, but charming voice proceeded to give his lecture in beautiful French. Looking up through his large gold spectacles (frightfully short-sighted), he said in reply to my question as to my studying at the Sorbonne: 'But we don't take little girls here,' perfectly amicably and beaming, 'You'll have to go across to the Collège de France to Rénan[12] and learn Hebrew and Semitic archaeology.'

....

10   *Egypt: papers and lectures by the late Mary Brodrick*, ed. E. Robinson (1938)
11   Sir Gaston Camille Charles Maspero, the leading French Egyptologist of his generation.
12   Joseph Ernest Renan, French Orientalist and Semitic scholar, author of the *Life of Jesus* (1863) which argued that Jesus was just a man, not a God, and rejected the miracles of the Gospels.

The 'little girl' was cheeky and pertinacious and maintained her intention of coming to learn. Maspero then said that there was going to be a Council meeting next Monday and he would inquire if it were possible for a woman to attend, and if they could admit me, I could have a talk to Rénan. I went then across to Rénan, and saw him coming back from a lecture. Rénan looked at me as though I were a black beetle and said: 'I have never taught a woman in my life, and I never will!' adding more gently that he was quite certain it was impossible but that if Maspero could admit me he would teach me.

I then went to ask what had happened at the Council meeting. Maspero said there was nothing in Richelieu's will[13] to prevent a woman from coming, so that I could come but that I should probably have a very bad time. However, I could try. I slipped in at the beginning of a lecture and sat at the back of the room. The [male] students gave me a bad time; they were rough and rude and they smelled. Just at first they teased me to no end, once pouring ink down my back; but I simply sat and laughed and in the end we became great friends, in some cases through life. [The group included] Legrain (the Archaeologist)[14], Groff (the Egyptologist)[15], Chassinat (the Scholar)[16], Benedite (Archaeologist and head of the Louvre)[17], and Philip Virey[18]. I studied Hebrew and Semitic archaeology and Roman law and history with Ernest Rénan, and Egyptology with Maspero, [and] the brothers Revilleut,[19] and Paul Pierret.[20] I worked at Groff's house at night, where he lived with his parents. The lodgings I had were in the Rue Singer, Passy, and the landlady would not give me food if I were late and so I often went without.

....

13   Cardinal Richelieu, former headmaster of the College of Sorbonne.
14   Georges Legrain, Curator and Excavator at the Temple of Karnak.
15   William N. Groff, American Egyptologist who lived in Cairo from 1891 to 1899.
16   Émile Gaston Chassinat, Director of the French Institute for Oriental Archaeology in Cairo.
17   Georges Aaron Bénédite, French Egyptologist and curator at the Louvre, discovered the Tomb of Akhethetep at Saqqara.
18   Philippe Virey, author of many books on Egyptian archaeology and culture.
19   One being Eugène Charles Revillout (1843–1913), professor of demotic, Coptic, and Egyptian law at the École du Louvre.
20   Curator at the Louvre, known for his translation of the Ancient Egyptian *Book of the Dead*.

After the course at the Sorbonne and at the Collège de France, I returned to London. Miss Grove of College Hall gave me a letter to Stuart Poole[21] of the British Museum, explaining that I wished to study archaeology. Renouf[22] was very good to me; he gravely handed me a hieroglyphic inscription and told me to take it home and transliterate and translate it. I racked my brains for days and nights—it was too difficult. I took it back humiliated and told Renouf that I could make nothing of it. The old man looked up with a charming smile and said: 'Neither can I,' and added that he had given it to me to see if I had any grit. He was very strict and made me look up references most carefully before committing myself in any way. Stuart Poole, Peter Renouf, and Sandy Murray[23]—these three old men—they were good to me. Later I was examined by the Keepers of the Greek Antiquities, Egyptian Antiquities, and of the Gems and Coins, and passed in all those subjects.[24] In 1888-89, I was appointed to deliver two courses of lectures and one set of demonstration classes on Roman Antiquities at the British Museum, and was the first [official] woman lecturer there."[25]

In her book, *Archaeologists in Print*, Amara Thornton writes, "... Brodrick was accepted to College Hall, the only residence for women university students in London... Brodrick received very little family support to pay for her residence at College Hall; the British Museum lectures provided her with much needed income and enabled her to remain based there. The Hall also served as her professional address where tickets for her lectures could be purchased. Like Helen Tirard [another female lecturer for the British Museum], Mary Brodrick charged for her course on 'Ancient Egyptian History and Antiquities', asking 21 shillings for the series and 4 shillings for a single lecture. Unlike Tirard's lectures, Brodrick's were open to both men and women (though predominantly attended by women), and were aimed particularly at those who had spent or anticipated spending time in Egypt...

....

21   Reginald Stuart Poole, Keeper of the Coins and Medals Department, British Museum
22   Peter le Page Renouf, keeper of the department of oriental antiquities at the British Museum.
23   Alexander Henry Hallam Murray, Brodrick's publisher
24   A notable exception from her tutors listed is that of Flinders Petrie, chair of Egyptology at the British Museum.
25   *Egypt: papers and lectures by the late Mary Brodrick*, ed. E. Robinson (1938), p. vii-xiii.

The visibility of these women was increasing in the press. In November the *Sheffield Daily Telegraph's* 'Lady Correspondent' highlighted the number of women writing and lecturing about Egypt, mentioning Tirard and Brodrick's efforts specifically. Brodrick, an open supporter of women's education, was clearly interested not only in the history of ancient Egypt, but particularly in women's experience of the ancient world... [She also gained respect in her field for translating key Egyptological works into English from German and French, revealing an impressive command of languages. One in particular, *Outlines of Ancient Egyptian History*, was the first time it was requested that she use her full name, Mary Brodrick, rather than M. Brodrick as usual, in order that her gender be clearly acknowledged and 'recognized'"].[26] Mary's journal records, "In 1893, I received the Ph.D. in Archaeology (University of Kansas)[27]; in 1897-1908, I worked in Egypt under Sir Gaston Maspero, Director of the Antiquity Department.[28] I lectured in Cairo frequently and also at intervals in England, Scotland, and Italy until 1932. In the winters I often had a dahabîyeh on the Nile, with my own crest-embroidered pennant flying. Interesting people sometimes came with me to visit historic places and to enjoy the dry, warm climate and the unique beauty of the Nile. Many were the happy, interesting parties—for artists, archaeologists, historians, and government officials came from other dahabîyehs and hotels to visit me. Keen discussions of every sort and kind took place, and the evenings often ended in delightful music."[29]

Robinson continues, "In March 1890 the American Charles Edwin Wilbour came across her in an all-women party on the *Gameeleh*, a steel-hulled dahabîyeh sometimes used by the Assyriologist Archibald H. Sayce (*Travels in Egypt*, 564). Brodrick recalled one incident at Luxor, when grave-robbers smuggled a mummy onto her dahabîyeh, at night and against her wishes, so that Maspero would not find it." A personal record by Brodrick regarding the event follows:

....

26   Thornton, Amara. *Archaeologists in Print: Publishing for the People*. London: UCL Press, 2018, p. 51-53
27   For her work in the U.S. as the English secretary for the Egypt Exploration Society
28   She also assisted in the opening of the famous Cairo Museum in 1902.
29   *Egypt: papers and lectures by the late Mary Brodrick*, ed. E. Robinson (1938), p. vii-xiii.

"The quiet Egyptian night had fallen as we moored to the bank a few miles from Luxor, safely tucked away from the barking of dogs and the inevitable ceaseless chatter of natives. I had retired about 10 pm to a peaceful spell of writing letters, making up notes of the day and such like odds and ends that one likes to do uninterruptedly and had said that no one was to come to me again.

Just as I had settled down comfortably to work, Samaan came to the cabin door to say that two Arabs wanted to speak to me and that they *must* see me as it was very important. Now I had made it a rule of the dahabîyeh that I would see no native after sunset. If it was anything good he had to say or anything he wanted, there were all the hours of daylight wherein he could come. It was a law like that of the Medes and Persians, to be unbroken, and the natives knew it. A stern negative was said and they were told to return in the morning, but, no, they absolutely refused to go. Long and loud were the arguments on both sides but still they remained. I had a grim suspicion that a little bakshish[30] was the cause of Samaan's reappearance:

'They say you know them quite well and they are good, and besides they won't go away.'

'Well, but who are they? They can't be on any good errand if they come at this time of night. Say I won't see them.'

More arguments and certainly bakshish in sufficient quantity to make it worth Samaan's while to again brave the wrath of the howadji[31], for once more he returned and pleaded the cause of the miscreants, adding that they were not fellahin [peasants], but certainly effendis [men of high social standing or learning].

I was very much puzzled as to whether to break a rule or to make an exception, but came to the conclusion, the country being a little unsettled at the moment, that on the whole it might be best to see

....
30   A Persian word, meaning payment (such as a tip or bribe) to expedite service. Merriam-Webster.
31   A Persian word, meaning a traveler in the East. 1913 Webster's Dictionary.

them. So moving the lamp to where it would fall on their faces I bade Samaan bring them in, but keep guard outside the door, ready to come in at once if wanted. The approaching footsteps were not those of low-class natives, the men coming along the little passage walked firmly and unafraid, and two tall completely shrouded figures came in and solemnly made obeisance [bowed]. I endeavored to look and speak as sternly as possible and demanded what right they had to set at naught the rule of 'Ellulu'. There was a momentary silence and, with a dramatic gesture both men then threw back their abbayas [cloaks] which they had pulled up over their heads, and stood proudly erect—two desert sheikhs of good Arab blood.

'You know us—we would never come to do you harm.'

'Ibrahim Mohammed and Selim Serani; what *are* you doing here? Speak at once!'

The men looked at each other and there was a curious, silent pause for several seconds, neither wishing to take the parable [speak] first.

At last Mohammed jerked out: 'There was a letter for you at the Luxor post office today, and we know that it means the Mudir of Antiquities is coming to see you.'

I blazed with fury at my letters having been seen and apparently examined at the Luxor post office, for it was quite true that the Director had written to tell me he would be in Luxor in a few days and asking me to go over to the other side of the river with him on my return.

At last I elicited from them, after much evasion and wriggling out of and circling around awkward questions, that they had been at the post office when the mail came in. The postmaster being a dear friend of theirs had jumped to the conclusion that the Director was coming, else why should he write to me, and warned them to hide any 'finds' at once. Now the Director had written my name and address in Arabic and signed the government envelope with the museum stamp as well, all of which upset their minds dreadfully. 'Very well,' said I, 'What does it matter to you if the Director is coming? It is inspection time; unless you have been breaking the law there is nothing to be afraid of.'

Two dithering voices answered: 'We have found a tomb and the mummy and what are we to do?' 'Will you buy the mummy, or shall we be put into prison?'—which certainly would happen.

Here was a situation fit for a shilling shocker, all the more so when the older man implored me to take the mummy up the river! I frankly confess I was in a thorough quandary. I was first of all angry that my letter had been the subject of discussion at the post office, and annoyed at being invited to the rescue of tomb-thieves, and yet, low be it spoken, my sympathies were with the two men. All sorts of promises had been made and every kind of inducement was at that moment being held out by the Antiquities Department to the natives to tell whenever or wherever there was anything found or even likely to be found, but I also knew that very often those promises were not fulfilled, with the result that things were separated and divided up and sold in different parts of Egypt. I also knew that some of the natives had been put in prison, and report had it, had been cruelly beaten to make them tell. The consequence was that a regular nefarious trade in antiquities was being carried on to the detriment of archaeology and the encouragement of the hazardous and most pernicious game of 'body-snatching'.

Said I, feeling very guilty, 'Bury the things in the sand.'

This they thought was a splendid idea and they would do it at night when no man saw, but what about the coffin and the mummy. Well, they would chop up the coffin and bury it out of sight and they supposed they had better pull the mummy to pieces and burn the body. At this I came down with force and threatened to hand them over to justice, or rather the ministers of the law.

A brilliant idea struck one of them. 'If you won't buy the mummy, will you take it and keep it till the Mudir has gone back to Cairo?' proceeding to explain that there was no moon and they would bring it over in a felucca [sailboat] with rags tied around the oars and no one would ever know. This met with a stern refusal. I was sorry all the same, for the men I felt that if they were caught, prison instead of reward would be their portion.

The lengthy argument and sustained refusal dragged on wearily until past midnight when, finding there was nothing to be hoped for and feeling thoroughly depressed, the two men cross the river to their homes at Abd el Gurneh[32] to cogitate upon the momentous question of how not to be found out, but I know in their secret hearts they were certain I would never give them away.

We were up betimes [early] the next morning with a north wind blowing, not a moment of which was to be lost. The siqala [anchor] had been hauled up and we were pulling out into midstream when my last night's visitors appeared on the bank and, with many gesticulations, yelled out in concert some information which the noise of the sailors and the general fuss of the start made it impossible to hear. Samaan had an odd, furtive look which was unusual and did not please me and there was obviously something not right.

There was an air of mystery about everybody which could not be accounted for; yet not all the most diplomatic ferreting could elicit anything. At last the [secret] had to come out. On the bunk in my spare cabin lay a beautifully-bound mummy, wrapped in the very finest linen—linen fine and soft as silk—the body evidently of some noble lord of Thebes who, in building his tomb in the Western desert believed that no eye would ever see him until the day when Osiris called him.

One's feelings at the moment are difficult to describe: rage that the tomb had been desecrated and the body disturbed, fury with those in my service who had played me this trick, and annoyance at the probable difficulties that would arise with the government if the robbery became known. After all, was I not in the position of an innocent receiver of stolen goods, and it was sacrilegious

----

32   Now Abd el-Qurna, located on the West Bank at Thebes in Upper Egypt.

besides? It was impossible to turn back; what was to be done? First of all, I close the cabin shutters and, covering the body with a sheet, locked the door and put the key in my pocket where it remained. Then I sent for every single soul on the dahabiyeh that was not actually needed for sailing, from the reis[33] down to the cook-boy. And they had such a castigation as frightened them thoroughly.

If they did not confess at once I would turn every man of them off at Aswân. Samaan and the reis were the ringleaders, undoubtedly, for this could not have happened without their connivance, and of course a huge bakshish. I wound up by saying that I must report it to the Mudir of Antiquities who would be at Luxor on our return, and, of course, everyone, Samaan included, would be sent to the convict prison in Cairo! Thereat I dismissed them and in blank consternation they returned to their duties.

I appears that those two Arabs, after they left me, got hold of the reis and Samaan and promised a very large reward if the mummy could be smuggled, unknown to me, on to the dahabîyeh, and there hidden until the return to Luxor, when it could be smuggled back to its finders. This seems to have been Samaan's brilliant idea; he argued that no one ever went into that cabin and so it would be quite safe to hide it there. The reis did not half like the plan, for he had been a long time with me, but the bakshish was too much a temptation and he weakly gave in. So in the dead of a moonless night these two arch-plotters took my felucca and with muffled oars, rowed across to the opposite bank, where the Arabs handed over the mummy which was eventually deposited on my spare-room bed.

It was a *very* chastened crew that went up to Aswan and a *most* chastened and depressed crew that returned to Luxor, where was the Director of Antiquities. Many were the prayers that I would save them from prison, and innumerable were the promises that never, no never, would they ever do such a thing again. All the bakshish they had receive would be placed at my feet if only I would not tell on them, etc.

....
33   Naval Captain

I kept them on tenterhooks and promised nothing. The Director duly came to see me on my return, and we had tea in the tiny saloon, he not realizing that only a thin wooden partition at his back separated him from the mummy, which a report said had been found and hidden by some Arabs, and which he had been vainly trying to locate. I never gave away either the Arabs, nor my iniquitous servants; as the hideous weeks of fright they went through while we remained at Luxor was punishment enough.

However, early one morning, when the sun was well up over the desert, the Director and I unwrapped *the body* [of one of the Lords of Ekhmîm, who had died and was buried at Thebes,] that lay shrouded on my bed in the exquisite linen for which Ekhmîm was famous."[34]

"Brodrick also kept in touch with Petrie, visiting him, for example, at the Egypt Exploration Society excavation at Dendera in winter 1897–8. She was closely involved with the Society for the Preservation of the Monuments of Ancient Egypt, a body first convened in August 1888 by the painter Edward Poynter. Poynter forwarded one of Brodrick's letters to *The Times*; in it she made a report of some of the problems faced in Egypt, noting, 'I caught two Egyptian soldiers in the act of cutting their names on the entrance of Aboo Simbel' (letter of 4 July 1890). Her observations had no doubt been made in the spring tour of that year mentioned by Wilbour. "[35]

Mary shares that, "Beshir Bey was head of the Beshari Tribes, and his cousin, Saledin Bey, had kept the wells at the time of the Gordon relief expedition. I was commissioned to take a signed portrait of Queen Victoria to Beshir Bey, acknowledging thereby his loyalty. Jocelin Woodhouse was Commandant at Assouan at the time. In 1898, I was made Life Member of the Bibliothèque Nationale, Paris; Member of the Advisory Council, and the Committee of Philology and Literary Archaeology at the

....

34   *Egypt Papers*, p. 118-123.
35   Gill, David. "Brodrick, Mary (1858–1933), archaeologist." *Oxford Dictionary of National Biography*. 23 Sep. 2004; Accessed 2 May. 2020. https://www.oxforddnb.com/view/10.1093/ref:odnb/9780198614128.001.0001/odnb-9780198614128-e-48602.

Columbian Internationale Exposition, and Life Member of College Hall, University of London. In 1899, I became Perpetual Member of La Comité de la Société Archéologique d'Egypt. In 1901 or 1902, there was a meeting and a luncheon party given to discuss the Cape to Cairo railway; Sir Samuel Baker, Sir Benjamin Baker, Lord Philip, Cromer, Kitchener, Cecil Rhodes, and myself...

It has been my good fortune to spend a great part of my life since 1888 in that fascinating country, Egypt, and to be brought into contact not only with British officials but with natives of both high and low degree, so I have been able to watch the development of that erstwhile chaotic country from those early days of our occupation when the post of H.M.'s Consul General for Egypt was one of all thorns and no roses and involved one perpetual struggle against bankruptcy, venality, disorder, hopeless inefficiency and inadequacy, to which were often added difficulties that arose from both European and local misunderstandings and even opposition."[36]

Thornton writes that, "Brodrick combined her work on the *A Handbook for Travellers in Lower and Upper Egypt* with a grueling public lecture schedule. In the late 1890's she was suffering with ill health, and as the new century dawned she was also struggling financially. A poignant letter in the John Murray archive reflects the lengths to which the Murrays [her publishers] were prepared to support her. In 1902 Anna Anderson Morton was preparing an application to the Royal Literary Fund on Brodrick's behalf; the Fund offered support to authors struggling financially. Even though she declared herself able to 'scrub along', Brodrick admitted, 'I do get dreadfully hampered now I am in such bad health.'

Her health increasingly forced her to give up valuable work opportunities. Following the publication of her and Morton's *Concise Dictionary* with Methuen & Co, Algernon Methuen had asked Brodrick to write another book on Egyptology, but she turned down the project. She explained to Murray that she was physically unable to 'chase out in all weathers to read at

....

36   *Egypt: papers and lectures by the late Mary Brodrick*, ed. E. Robinson (1938), p. vii-xiii.

the museum', and could not afford to buy 'essential' reference works or arrange trips to museums abroad for other necessary information. She outlined her financial circumstances as an independent author and lecturer—added to her £70 a year of money through the Brodrick family, were her literary earnings of about £100 a year 'according to luck + health'. A later letter reveals that the Murray brothers worked behind the scenes to ensure that she received a grant of £50 from the Fund in 1903. She recalled in this letter that, despite her outlined earnings, 'there were several years where "ends" would hardly meet.' When Brodrick later came into money she made a donation back to the Fund, in order to ensure other authors might receive help at difficult times; the Fund wrote a specific note detailing the donation was for its 'help in time of misfortune'. [Indeed Brodrick's worth was valued at £46352 (~$55,584 US dollars) when she died, and much of it was given away.]

Throughout the correspondence it is clear that as an author Mary Brodrick acted on her own initiative; she took on her critics and used the benefit of her experience and contacts to improve Murray's [*Guide*] for tourists. Brodrick's correspondence shows the strength of the relationship between archaeologist and publisher during this period—one that was quite personal, as evident in the Murray brothers' financial support during and after her work on the *Handbook*. While they did not support her every publishing effort, the brothers, particularly Hallam Murray, worked to cultivate Brodrick as an author or lecturer, offering her opportunities, promotion, and funding when she requested them, and when she did not."[37]

Robinson concludes, "There can be little doubt that it was at this time that she attended the Gordon Memorial service and took the 'Salute' of which she spoke to several of her friends. In 1913, she was made Dame of Grace of the Order of St. John of Jerusalem, and Fellow of the Geographical Society, England (honorary). On January 11, 1918, she lectured at the Kensington Town Hall for the Royal Geographical Society, Sir Thomas Holdich, President, in

....

37   Thornton, Amara. *Archaeologists in Print: Publishing for the People*. London: UCL Press, 2018, p. 140-141.

the chair. In 1925, she became Honorary Fellow of the American Geographical Society, and in 1927, Member of the Geographical Society of America, Washington.

When May Brodrick talked of Egypt, her audiences were wafted away from all present surroundings into the ages of the past. The whole expression of her face changed as though she were actually there, in the warm dry air, the glowing, glittering sand with the indescribable sunsets, and the roll up of the deep blue mantle of night. On the Blue Nile with its boats like strange beautiful birds, their crossed white wings reflecting the colors of the passing day; in the distance the squeals of the water wheels (*saqiyas*) as turned laboriously by bullock, camel, or donkey while they poured their water onto the fields, while the '*shadufs*' whose water pots at the end of long poles were slung high up on the fields, in silence. In a little hollow in the sand, she had sometimes slept in her camel hair bag, and, waking, watched the stars and felt the little wind at dawn that crept across the desert like a multitude of fairy feet bringing winged messages of inspiration and delight.

Deep in her heart she felt the immensity, mystery, and silence of the desert, as well as of this ancient people whose history, philosophy, and knowledge were only gradually emerging from the silence of the centuries. They had left their impress on mankind in the beauty of their art, thought, and learning, but the source of it had been lost for many ages. It was only now, by means of the work a few pioneers of determination and genius that the world was awakening to the immensity and importance of this old Egyptian civilization. People, places, and things rose again as the lecturer described them with punctilious accuracy, clearness, humor, and insight into character. The dry bones of the past awoke again to life as she caught their spirit and clothed them with imagination, tempered by patient historical research. With powerful description and imitable voice and language, she carried all who listened deep into the lives of these many-thousand-year-old people, till they seemed to live and breathe again, almost as they themselves had firmly expected to do so."[38]

....

38 *Egypt: papers and lectures by the late Mary Brodrick*, ed. E. Robinson (1938), p. vii-xiii.

Mentions and Remembrances of Mary Brodrick

"Miss Mary Brodrick, Ph.D., who is delivering a series of lectures on Ancient Egypt in the British Museum, knows that country better than any living woman. Her acquaintance with it dates back to the winter of 1888, and she has lived there more or less ever since. **Her indefatigable energy in archaeological research has greatly increased our knowledge of the history, religion, and architecture of the ancient inhabitants of that country.** Mr. Murray, of Handbook fame, commissioned her to write his latest guide to Egypt—a most scholarly and at the same time practical work."~ *Unknown*

"A GREAT LADY EGYPTOLOGIST. **Miss Brodrick is perhaps the greatest lady Egyptologist of the day.** She has spent more than twenty years in the land of the Pharaohs, giving up her time entirely to research. A few years ago the [University of Kansas] conferred the degree of Doctor of Philosophy, *honoris causa*, upon her. Miss Brodrick is also well known as a lecturer at the British Museum." ~ *Daily Mail*, 26 November 1906

"**This is May Brodrick as her friends will ever think of her——a live wire—generous in mind and utterly free from petty jealousy, with a genius for friendship.** She herself believed that she had accomplished so little. The truth is that she had hitched her wagon to the stars and could never rest satisfied with less than the best. **She was as unconscious of the value of her example as she was of the milestones of kind acts that marked the path she had traversed."** ~ (Signed) Hilda Keppel[39]

An appreciation in *The Times* (22 July 1933) noted her 'fine head and brow, with its upstanding short white hair, keen eyes, and vivid smile, the spare form always clothed in black'.[40]

....

39   Lady Hilda Mary Keppel, daughter of William Keppel, 7th Earl of Albemarle
40   Gill, David. "Brodrick, Mary (1858–1933), archaeologist." *Oxford Dictionary of National Biography*. 23 Sep. 2004; Accessed 2 May. 2020.

"Haslemere[41] attracts many people of eminence and of striking appearance, but **Miss Brodrick would usually be one of the most striking appearance in any assembly. She belonged to the company of rare souls who are as much above the limitations and characteristics of [gender] as they are above dogma, who are found in any religion, like Dante and St. Francis, like Baron Von Hugel and Israel Abrahams; whose presence is a rebuke to sin and silliness and pedantry and narrowness. It was not a presumption to love her, but it would have been a condemnation not to.**" ~ Ulric Gantillon, late Syriac Professor at Oxford.

"Princess Alice, Countess of Athlone, was given a great welcome by women students when she visited College Hall, Malet-Street, yesterday to open the Mary Brodrick wing. The new building for College Hall was opened only two years ago by the Queen, and the further rapid extension was made possible by a legacy from the late Dr. Mary Brodrick, one of the first students to enter College Hall 52 years ago. Sir Alexander Gibb, chairman of the council, with Lord Daryngton, the treasurer, were among those who received Princess Alice, and there were presented to her Royal Highness the founders of the original hall—Lady Lockyer, Miss Leigh Browne, and Miss. M.S. Kilgour. The new wing provides 60 study bedrooms, together with a new council room, additional provision for common rooms, a games room, and a new students' laundry. In a special room—called the Mary Brodrick room— were her portrait and various personal belongings." ~ *The Daily Telegraph*, London, 16 Nov. 1934.

"It is not only as a benefactor that we commemorate her, she was among the most distinguished that belonged to us. **She was one of the best-known pioneer women Egyptologists.**" ~ Extract from Dr. Louisa Macdonald's Address at College Hall, London, November, 1933.
"In the recent death of Miss Mary Brodrick, Ph.D., F.R.G.S., College Hall has lost one of its most distinguished Old Students and one of **the kindest, wisest, most generous and true of friends.**" ~ *The Times*, July 22, 1933.

....

41   Town in Surrey, England

Publications by Mary Brodrick

- *Egypt Under the Pharaohs: A History Derived Entirely from the Monuments*, By Heinrich Brugsch-Bey, John Murray, London, 1891 (As Translator and Editor)

- *Outlines of Ancient Egyptian History,* By Auguste Mariette, John Murray, London, 1892. (As Translator and Editor)

- *A Handbook for Travellers in Lower and Upper Egypt*, 9th edition. John Murray, London, 1896. (As Editor) (also 10th edition, 1900)

- "The Tomb of Pepu ankh (khua), near Sharona". Proceedings of the Society of Biblical Archaeology, 21 (1899), pp. 26–33. (With Anna Anderson Morton) (1899)

- *The Life and Confession of Asenath, The Daughter of Pentephres of Heliopolis Narrating How The All-Beautiful Joseph Took Her To Wife.* P. Wellby, London, 1900. (As Translator, with Peter Le Page Renouf)

- *A Concise Dictionary of Egyptian Archaeology: A Handbook for Students and Travellers.* Methuen, London, 1902. (With Anna Anderson Morton)

- *A Handbook for Travellers in Syria and Palestine,* Revised edition. Edward Stanford, London, 1903. (As Editor)

- *The Trial and Crucifixion of Jesus Christ of Nazareth.* John Murray, London, 1908.

- *Egypt: Papers and Lectures by the Late Mary Brodrick.* De La More Press, London, 1937. (Selected and edited by Eversley Robinson)

- *Various Articles and Addresses*:
  - The Authenticity of Sacred Sites
  - The Bellfounders and Carillons of Belgium
  - College Hall in the Early Nineties, 1927
  - Our Inheritance, 1827-1927, 1936
  - Failure and Effort, 1928
  - Unity and Uniformity, 1930
  - Retrospect and Prospect, Farewell and All Hail, 1932

Part Two

Blended Scriptural Sequence of Events
by the Editor, confirmed by Brodrick

A Chronologically Integrated Gospel Record of Jesus' Various Trials, Crucifixion, and Burial.

Who's who:

King Herod Antipas: Reigned 4 B.C. – A.D. 39 as the King of Judea over the Jewish people. He was the son of Herod the Great who beheaded John the Baptist. Jesus called him a "fox" in Luke 13:32.

Annas: One of the High Priests of Jerusalem, from A.D. 6-7 to A.D. 15. Continued to be known by the title of High Priest (Lk. 3:2, Acts 4:6) for the rest of his life. His son-in-law Caiaphas officially presided over Jesus' trial.

Caiaphas: High Priest appointed in A.D. 18. Member of the Sadducees, called for Jesus' death after He raised Lazarus from the dead.

Sanhedrin: The highest ruling body and court of justice among the Jewish people. Headed by the high priest of Israel, the Sanhedrin was granted limited authority over certain religious, civil, and criminal matters by Rome. It charged Jesus with the crime of blasphemy, but Pilate had to be the one to pronounce death. Some of the more well-known members of the Sanhedrin were Joseph of Arimathea (Mk. 15:43), Gamaliel (Acts 5:34), Nicodemus (John 3:1, 7:50), Ananias (Acts 23:2) and of course, Annas and Caiaphas (Lk. 3:2). The Sanhedrin even had its own police force, or Temple police (the *shoterim*), so it could make arrests on its own. This is the force that arrested Jesus in the Garden of Gethsemane (Mk. 14:43, Acts 4:1-3). (*Nelson's New Illustrated Bible Dictionary*, p. 1127-1128.)

Pontius Pilate: Roman prefect of Judea, reigned AD 26-36. He governed the Roman citizens and was not popular with the Jews, which may have been the reason he was willing to give them what they wanted—the crucifixion of Jesus—despite his own feelings about it.

1. **Annas questions Jesus privately first, Peter denies first time, Thursday Night. (John 18:12-24)**

So the band of soldiers and their captain and the officers of the Jews arrested Jesus and bound Him. First they led Him to Annas, for he was the father-in-law of Caiaphas, who was high priest that year. [...] The high priest then questioned Jesus about His disciples and His teaching. Jesus answered him, "I have spoken openly to the world. I have always taught in synagogues and in the temple, where all Jews come together. I have said nothing in secret. Why do you ask Me? Ask those who have heard Me what I said to them; they know what I said." When He had said these things, one of the officers standing by struck Jesus with his hand, saying, "Is that how you answer the high priest?" Jesus answered him, "If what I said is wrong, bear witness about the wrong; but if what I said is right, why do you strike Me?" Annas then sent Him bound to Caiaphas the high priest.

2. **Secret trial with Caiaphas (Matt. 26:59-75, Mark 14:55-72, Luke 22:54-65, John 18:25-27), Jesus is beaten, Peter denies 2 more times.[42] Late Thursday night /early Friday morning.**

Now the chief priests, elders, and whole council were seeking false testimony against Jesus that they might put Him to death, but they found none. For while many bore false witness against Him, their testimony did not agree with each other. At last two came forward and said, "We heard Him say, 'I will destroy this temple that is made with hands, and in three days I will build another, not made with hands.'" Yet even about this their testimony did not agree. And the high priest stood up in the midst and asked Jesus, "Have You no answer to make? What is it that these

....

42   Very late Thursday night to very early Friday morning (rooster crowed), perhaps sometime between 12 midnight - 3am.... sometimes there is confusion on whether the courtyard where Peter denied Christ was at Annas' residence or at Caiaphas' residence (compare Matthew and John's account). But it is possible that since the two men (Annas and Caiaphas) were family they shared the same estate or complex, thus shared the same courtyard. So, though Annas sent Jesus bound to Caiaphas they remained in the same courtyard where Peter denied the Lord through both Annas and Caiaphas's interrogation of Jesus.

men testify against You?" But He remained silent and made no answer. Again the high priest asked Him, "Are you the Christ, the Son of the Blessed?" Jesus said to him, "I am, as you have said. But I tell you, from now on you will see the Son of Man seated at the right hand of the power of God and coming on the clouds of heaven." And the high priest tore his garments and said, "He has uttered blasphemy. What further witnesses do we need? You have heard His blasphemy from His own lips. What is your decision?" And they all condemned Him as deserving death. Now the men who were holding Jesus in custody were mocking Him as they beat Him. They spit in His face and struck Him, the guards received Him with blows, and they also blindfolded Him and some slapped Him, saying, "Prophesy to us, you Christ! Who is it that struck You?" And they said many other things against Him, blaspheming Him.

3. **Sanhedrin Condemnation, Friday morning (Luke 22:66-71, Matt. 27:1, Mark 15:1a), Judas commits suicide (Matt 27:3-10)**

When day came, the assembly of the elders of the people gathered together, both chief priests and scribes. And they led Him away to their council, and they said, "If You are the Christ, tell us." But He said to them, "If I tell you, you will not believe, and if I ask you, you will not answer. But from now on the Son of Man shall be seated at the right hand of the power of God." So they all said, "Are you the Son of God, then?" And He said to them, "You say that I am." Then they said, "What further testimony do we need? We have heard it ourselves from His own lips." Then all the chief priests and the elders of the people took counsel against Jesus to put Him to death. And they bound Him and led Him away and delivered Him over to Pilate the governor.

4. **Before Pilate, Friday morning (Matt. 27:1-14; Mark 15:1b-5; Luke 23:1-7, John 18:28-32)**

Then they led Jesus from the house of Caiaphas to the governor's headquarters. It was early morning. They themselves did not enter the governor's headquarters, so that they would not be defiled, but could eat the Passover. So Pilate went outside to them and said, "What accusation do you bring against this Man?" They answered him, "If this Man were not doing evil, we would not have delivered Him over to you." Pilate said to them, "Take Him yourselves and judge Him by your own law." The Jews said to him, "It is not lawful for us to put anyone to death." This was to fulfill the word that Jesus had spoken to show by what kind of death He was going to die.

And Pilate asked Him, "Are you the King of the Jews?" And He answered him, "You have said so." And they began to accuse Him, saying, "We found this Man misleading our nation and forbidding us to give tribute to Caesar (cf. Mark 12:17), and saying that He Himself is Christ, a king." And Pilate again asked Him, "Have You no answer to make? See how many charges they bring against You." But Jesus made no further answer, so that Pilate was amazed.

Then Pilate said to the chief priests and the crowds, "I find no guilt in this Man." But they were urgent, saying, "He stirs up the people, teaching throughout all Judea, from Galilee even to this place." When Pilate heard this, he asked whether the Man was a Galilean. And when he learned that He belonged to Herod's jurisdiction, he sent Him over to Herod, who was himself in Jerusalem at that time.

5. Sent to Herod, Friday morning (Luke 23:8-12)

When Herod saw Jesus, he was very glad, for he had long desired to see Him, because he had heard about Him, and he was hoping to see some sign done by Him. So he questioned Him at some length, but He made no answer. The chief priests and the scribes stood by, vehemently accusing Him. And Herod with his soldiers treated Him with contempt and mocked Him. Then, arraying Him in splendid clothing, he sent Him back to Pilate. And Herod and Pilate became friends with each other that very day, for before this they had been at enmity with each other.

6. Back to Pilate (Matt. 27:15-26, Mark 15:6-15, Luke 23:13-25, John 18:33-19:16a), Jesus is scourged and beaten. Still Friday morning.

So Pilate entered his headquarters again and called Jesus and said to Him, "Are You the King of the Jews?" Jesus answered, "Do you say this of your own accord, or did others say it to you about Me?" Pilate answered, "Am I a Jew? Your own nation and the chief priests have delivered You over to me. What have You done?" Jesus answered, "My kingdom is not of this world. If My kingdom were of this world, My servants would have been fighting, that I might not be delivered over to the Jews. But My kingdom is not from the world." Then Pilate said to Him, "So You are a king?" Jesus answered, "You say that I am a king. For this purpose I was born and for this purpose I have come into the world—to bear witness to the truth. Everyone who is of the truth listens to My voice." Pilate said to Him, "What is truth?"

After he had said this, he went back outside. Pilate then called together the chief priests and the rulers and the people, and said to them, "You brought me this Man as One who was misleading the people. And after examining Him before you, behold, I did not find this Man guilty of any of your charges against Him. Neither did Herod, for he sent Him back to us. Look, nothing deserving death has been done by Him. I will therefore punish and release Him." Now at the feast the governor was accustomed to release for the crowd any one prisoner whom they wanted. And they had then a notorious prisoner called Barabbas. So when they had gathered, Pilate said to them, "Whom do you want me to release for you: Barabbas, or Jesus Who is called Christ?"

For he perceived that it was out of envy that the chief priests had delivered him up. Besides, while he was sitting on the judgment seat, his wife sent word to him, "Have nothing to do with that righteous man, for I have suffered much because of him today in a dream."

They cried out, "Not this Man, but Barabbas!" Now Barabbas was a robber. And Pilate again said to them, "Then what shall I do with the Man you call the King of the Jews?" And they cried out again, "Crucify Him." And Pilate said to them, "Why? What evil has He done?" But they shouted all the more, "Crucify Him." So Pilate, wishing to satisfy the crowd, released for them Barabbas, and took Jesus and flogged Him.

So the soldiers led Him away inside the palace (that is, the governor's headquarters), and they called together the whole battalion. And they clothed Him in a purple cloak, and twisting together a crown of thorns, they put it on Him. They came up to Him, saying, "Hail, King of the Jews!" and struck Him with their hands. And they were striking His head with a reed and spitting on Him and kneeling down in homage to Him. And when they had mocked Him, they stripped Him of the purple cloak and put His own clothes on Him.

Pilate went out again and said to them, "See, I am bringing Him out to you that you may know that I find no guilt in Him." So Jesus came out, wearing the crown of thorns and the purple robe. Pilate said to them, "Behold the Man!" When the chief priests and the officers saw Him, they cried out, "Crucify Him, crucify Him!" So when Pilate saw that he was gaining nothing, but rather that a riot was beginning, he took water and washed his hands before the crowd, saying, "I am innocent of this Man's blood; Take Him yourselves and crucify Him, for I find no guilt in Him."

And all the people answered, "His blood be on us and on our children! We have a law, and according to that law He ought to die because He has made Himself the Son of God." When Pilate heard this statement, he was even more afraid. He entered his headquarters again and said to Jesus, "Where are you from?" But Jesus gave him no answer. So Pilate said to Him, "You will not speak to me? Do you not know that I have authority to release You and authority to crucify You?" Jesus answered him, "You would have no authority over Me at all unless it had been given you from above. Therefore he who delivered Me over to you has the greater sin."

From then on Pilate sought to release Him, but the Jews cried out, "If you release this Man, you are not Caesar's friend. Everyone who makes Himself a king opposes Caesar." So when Pilate heard these words, he brought Jesus out and sat down on the judgment seat at a place called 'The Stone Pavement', and in Aramaic 'Gabbatha'. Now it was the day of Preparation of the Passover. It was about the sixth hour. He said to the Jews, "Behold your King!" They cried out, "Away with Him, away with Him, crucify Him!" Pilate said to them, "Shall I crucify your King?" The chief priests answered, "We have no king but Caesar." So he delivered Him over to them to be crucified.

7. **The Crucifixion, 9am Friday morning (Matt. 27:31-56, Mark 15:20-41, Luke 23:26-49, John 19:16b-37)**

When they had mocked Him, they stripped Him of the purple robe, put His clothes on Him, and led Him out to crucify Him. As they were going out, they forced a man coming in from the country, who was passing by, to carry Jesus' cross. He was Simon, a Cyrenian, the father of Alexander and Rufus.

A large crowd of people followed Him, including women who were mourning and lamenting Him. But turning to them, Jesus said, "Daughters of Jerusalem, do not weep for Me, but weep for yourselves and *your children. Look, the days are coming when they will say, 'The women without children, the wombs that never bore and the breasts that never nursed, are fortunate!' Then they will begin to say to the mountains, 'Fall on us!' and to the hills, 'Cover us!' For if they do these things when the wood is green, what will happen when it is dry?"*

Two others—criminals—were also led away to be executed with Him. When they arrived at [In the Hebrew] Golgotha [Latin: Calvary] a place called the place of a skull, *they tried to give Him wine mixed with myrrh[43], but He did not take it. Then they crucified Him. Now it was nine in the morning when they crucified Him. Then Jesus said, "Father, forgive them, because they do not know what they are doing."*

Pilate also had a sign lettered and put on the cross. The inscription of the charge written against Him was:

THIS IS JESUS OF NAZARETH. THE KING OF THE JEWS.

Many of the Jews read this sign, because the place where Jesus was crucified was near the city, and it was written in Hebrew, Latin, and Greek. So the chief priests of the Jews said to Pilate, "Don't write, 'The King of the Jews,' but that He said, 'I am the King of the Jews.'" Pilate replied, "What I have written, I have written."

When the soldiers crucified Jesus, they took His clothes and divided them into four parts, a part for each soldier. They also took the tunic, which was seamless, woven in one piece from the top. So they said to one another, "Let's not tear it, but cast lots for it, to see who gets it." They did this to fulfill the Scripture that says: They divided My clothes among themselves, and they cast lots for My clothing[44]. *And this is what the soldiers did.*

They crucified two criminals with Him, one on His right and one on His left. So the Scripture was fulfilled that says: And He was counted among outlaws.[45] *Those who passed by were yelling insults at Him, shaking their heads, and saying, "Ha! The One who would demolish the sanctuary and build it in three days, save Yourself by coming down from the cross!" In*

....

43   Ps. 69:21
44   Ps. 22:18
45   Is. 53:12

the same way, the chief priests with the scribes were mocking Him to one another and saying, "He saved others; He cannot save Himself! Let the Messiah, the King of Israel, come down now from the cross, so that we may see and believe. He has put His trust in God; let God rescue Him now—if He wants Him! For He said, 'I am God's Son.'"

Then one of the criminals hanging there began to yell insults at Him: "Aren't You the Messiah? Save Yourself and us!" But the other answered, rebuking him: "Don't you even fear God, since you are undergoing the same punishment? We are punished justly, because we're getting back what we deserve for the things we did, but this Man has done nothing wrong." Then he said, "Jesus, remember me when You come into Your kingdom!" And He said to him, "I assure you: Today you will be with Me in paradise."

Standing by the cross of Jesus were His mother, His mother's sister, Mary the wife of Cleophas, and Mary Magdalene. When Jesus saw His mother and the disciple He loved standing there, He said to His mother, "Woman, here is your son." Then He said to the disciple, "Here is your mother." And from that hour the disciple took her into his home.

From noon until three in the afternoon darkness came over the whole land, because the sun's light failed. About three in the afternoon Jesus cried out with a loud voice, "Elí, Elí, lemá sabachtháni?" that is, "My God, My God, why have You forsaken Me?"[46] When some of those standing there heard this, they said, "He's calling for Elijah!"

After this, when Jesus knew that everything was now accomplished that the Scripture might be fulfilled, He said, "I thirst!"[47]

A jar full of sour wine was sitting there; immediately one of them ran and got a sponge, filled it with sour wine on hyssop, fixed it on a reed and held it up to His mouth. But the rest said, "Let's see if Elijah comes to save Him!"

When Jesus had received the sour wine, He called out with a loud voice, "Father, into Your hands I entrust My spirit. It is finished!"

....

46   Ps. 22:1
47   Ps. 69:21

Then bowing His head, He breathed His last and gave up His spirit.

Suddenly, the curtain of the sanctuary was split in two from top to bottom; the earth quaked and the rocks were split. The tombs were also opened and many bodies of the saints who had fallen asleep were raised. And they came out of the tombs after His resurrection, entered the holy city, and appeared to many.

When the centurion and those with him, who were guarding Jesus, saw the earthquake and the things that had happened, they were terrified and said, "This Man really was God's Son!"

All the crowds that had gathered for this spectacle, when they saw what had taken place, went home, striking their chests. But all who knew Him, including the women who had followed Him from Galilee, stood at a distance, watching these things. Among them were Mary Magdalene, Mary the mother of James and Joseph, and the mother of Zebedee's sons. Since it was the preparation day, the Jews did not want the bodies to remain on the cross on the Sabbath (for that Sabbath was a special day). They requested that Pilate have the men's legs broken and that their bodies be taken away. So the soldiers came and broke the legs of the first man and of the other one who had been crucified with Him. When they came to Jesus, they did not break His legs since they saw that He was already dead. But one of the soldiers pierced His side with a spear, and at once blood and water came out. He who saw this has testified so that you also may believe. His testimony is true, and he knows he is telling the truth. For these things happened so that the Scripture would be fulfilled: Not one of His bones will be broken.[48] Also, another Scripture says: They will look at the One they pierced.[49]

8. **The Burial, between 3pm and sundown, Friday afternoon/ early evening (Matt. 27:57-66, Mark 15:42-47, Luke 23:50-56, John 19:38-42)**

When it was already evening, because it was preparation day (that is, the day before the Sabbath), Joseph of Arimathea [a Judean town], a good and righteous man, a prominent member of the Sanhedrin who was himself looking forward to the kingdom of God, and who was a disciple of Jesus—

....

48   Ps 34:20
49   Zech 12:10

but secretly because of his fear of the Jews—came and boldly went in to Pilate and asked for Jesus' body. Pilate was surprised that He was already dead. Summoning the centurion, he asked him whether He had already died. When he found out from the centurion, Pilate ordered that [the body] be released to Joseph.

After [Joseph] bought some fine linen, he took Him down off the cross. There was a garden in the place where He was crucified. A new tomb was in the garden cut out of the rock; no one had yet been placed in it. It was preparation day, and the Sabbath was about to begin. They placed Jesus there because of the Jewish preparation and since the tomb was nearby. Nicodemus (who had previously come to Jesus at night) also came, bringing a mixture of about 75 pounds of myrrh and aloes. Then they took Jesus' body and wrapped it in the linen cloths with the aromatic spices, according to the burial custom of the Jews. Joseph left after rolling a great stone against the entrance of the tomb.

Now Mary Magdalene and Mary the mother of Joseph were seated there, facing the tomb, watching where He was placed. Then they returned and prepared spices and perfumes. And they rested on the Sabbath according to the commandment.

The next day [Saturday], which followed the preparation day, the chief priests and the Pharisees gathered before Pilate and said, "Sir, we remember that while this deceiver was still alive He said, 'After three days I will rise again.' Therefore give orders that the tomb be made secure until the third day. Otherwise, His disciples may come, steal Him, and tell the people, 'He has been raised from the dead.' Then the last deception will be worse than the first." "You have a guard of soldiers," Pilate told them. "Go and make it as secure as you know how." Then they went and made the tomb secure by sealing the stone and setting the guard.

Part Three

*The Trial and Crucifixion of
Jesus Christ of Nazareth*

The 1908 work by Mary Brodrick,
edited for a modern audience

The Trial and Crucifixion of Jesus Christ of Nazareth

By M. Brodrick
London: John Murray, Albemarle Street 1908

Preface

The following pages are the substance of lectures which have been delivered at various times and in many places other than the United Kingdom, and it is in response to the request of many members of my audiences to possess them in permanent form that I venture to publish them.

They are purely historical and legal, and the subject has been purposely treated from a formal and prosaic [factual] standpoint. The four Gospels alone are their basis, and thus many traditions and hypotheses which bear the stamp of possibility are ignored as not sufficiently capable of proof. The statements made about the Jews may at first sight appear to be somewhat severe, but they can be proved both from the Gospels and secular history, and, of course, only apply to the people as they were in the days of Christ. There are many references to both Jewish and English writers which I should like to have given; but illness and enforced absence from England have prevented me from consulting the authors themselves, and giving the exact chapter and section of their works.

On page 39 reference is made to the 40 vols, of the Talmud. *The Editio Princeps*, however, is in 12 vols., and an edition of 1664, published in Amsterdam, is printed in 19 vols.

There are also editions of the Mishna in 3 vols. and 6 vols. as well as that in 12 vols.

I have therefore not attempted to put the lectures into literary shape, but have left them in the colloquial form in which they were given, trusting that with all their failings they may not be found unhelpful to a sober and accurate realization of the last day of our Lord's pre-Resurrection life.

Bordighera, 1908.

Mary Brodrick

M. B.

Books Referred to by the Author

* Carini, *Passione diChristo*.
* Cassiodorus, *Chronicles*.
* Castelli, *La legge del popolo ebreo*.
* Cicero, *Letter to Verres; Pro Rabirio*.
* *Dictionary of the Bible* (Hastings).
* Eusebius, *Life of Constantine; Praise of Constantine; On the Theophania*.
* Gatti, *Album de Rossi*.
* Harnack, *History of Dogma*.
* Josephus, *Antiquities of the Jews; Wars of the Jews*.
* Keim, *Jesus von Nazara*.
* Levi, *Sulla teocrazzia mosaica*.
* Maimonides, *De Synedriis*.
* Migne, *Patrologia Graeca; Patrologia Latina*.
* Mommsen, *Provinces de Rome de César à Dioclétian*.
* *Palestine Exploration Fund Quarterly Statements*.
* *Palestine Pilgrims' Texts*.
* Petrucelli della Gattina, *Memorie di Giuda*.
* Rabbinowicz, *Législation criminelle du Talmud*.
* Renan, *Histoire du peuple d'Israël*.
* Roman, *Penal Code*.
* Salvador, *Histoire des institutions de Moïse et du peuple*
* *Hébreu; La loi de Moïse*.
* Schürer, *History of the Jewish People*.
* Schwab, *Le Talmud de Jérusalem*.
* Suetonius, *Lives of the Cæsars*.
* Tacitus, *Annals*.
* Talmud, *Of Babylon*.
* Talmud, *Of Jerusalem*.
* Taylor Innes, *The Trial of Jesus Christ*.
* Wilson, *Golgotha and the Holy Sepulchre*

Lecture I: The Arrest

<u>Topics Covered</u>: The Arrest, Purpose of the Book, Testimony of Josephus, The Purpose of Christ's Ministry, the Censure of Pharisees and Sadducees, the Mission of Jesus: Reformation Not Revolution, a Prolegomena of Jewish History, the Popular Expectation of the Messiah, Two Opposing Forces (Pharisees and Sadducees), Attempts on the Life of Christ, the Courage and Acumen of Nicodemus, the Advice of Caiaphas, the Question of the Legality of the Meeting, the Actual Arrest, the Identification of the Temple Guard, the Illegality of the Arrest, the Peculiarities of Jewish Law, the Talmud, the Work of the Rabbis, the Sanhedrin, the Composition of the Court, the Time of Session, the Pharisees, the Sadducees, and the Scribes.

THE ARREST

On three things stand the world — on Law, on Worship, and on Charity.

The closing scenes of the life of Jesus Christ are familiar to us all; in a certain sense they are almost too familiar, for we have heard them read and preached upon so often, that though the words reach our ears I think they sometimes fail to penetrate our brain.

It is possible to read the New Testament until it is taken for granted, instead of being known intelligently — to read it with the spirit, yet not with the understanding.

For some people it is sufficient to accept the fact that Christ's condemnation and death were unjust, and to contemplate them from their theological and spiritual aspect; but there are also a great many who are not content to give a mere spiritual acquiescence in a belief, the result of which has altered the whole course of humanity. They desire to know from a historical point of view *why* the Jews were so relentless in their persecution of the new Teacher, and from a legal point of view *how* the law of Israel was set aside.

Much has been written concerning the last hours of our Lord's life, chiefly from their devotional and theological point of view, but from the legal and purely human aspect there is not much in popular form as the works of the best authorities are technical, and not easily within the reach of the general reader.

The whole story is a wondrously human document. It is nothing less than the trial of a Hebrew Citizen in the sacred city itself, and before the highest tribunal in Jewry, upon a count so grave that if it could be proved, nothing but the utmost penalty of the law awaited Him, and carried out with all speed after the delivery of the sentence. A sentence from which there could be no appeal. Every Christian knows that the arrest of Christ was illegal, His trial conducted unjustly, His condemnation and death nothing short of deliberate murder; but how many could clearly state where the Jewish law miscarried? All will admit that Pontius Pilate failed to administer the Roman law with uprightness and justice, yet in what manner did he fail? All will acknowledge that the punishment of crucifixion was a lingering and painful one, yet how many could accurately describe, even if they knew correctly, the method of its infliction?

PURPOSE OF THE BOOK

What I propose to do in these lectures is to ask you to examine carefully and in sequence the various details of our Lord's trial and death, and I think you will agree that only by a comparison of the Gospels with Jewish and Roman law, can we appreciate, or even in one or two instances understand, Christ's attitude before His accusers.

Further, that there shall arise no misunderstandings between us, let me make it quite clear that everything will be looked at from the *human* standpoint alone. I shall in no way trench upon theology or dogma, nor upon any points connected with the Divine Nature of our Lord. All terms used will bear their literal sense, and everything that touches upon the religious side of the subject will be eliminated.

We will look at the events, as they took place, in the dry, clear light of law and history and in a strictly formal method.

TESTIMONY OF JOSEPHUS

Our *historical* data will be the four Gospels, the only authentic contemporaneous records that we have at present;[50] of classical allusions to Jesus Christ there are — so far as I know — only two direct ones, those of Josephus the Jew and Tacitus the Roman, though there are indirect allusions to the founder of the Christian religion in Suetonius, Lucian, Pliny the Elder, and Epictetus. Here and there throughout the Talmud, there are also references to him couched in derogatory terms, but of no value historically, and I believe they have been suppressed by the Censor in modern printed copies.

Josephus says, "At that time lived Jesus, a wise Man, if He could be called wise. He did marvelous things, and was the Master of those men who received the truth with joy. He, moreover, brought over many Jews to His side as also many foreigners of the Greek countries. This was the Christ. When, on the accusation of the most influential men among us, Pilate sentenced Him to death on the cross, His followers nevertheless did not forsake Him. He appeared among them on the third day, because divine prophecies had foretold of Him this, and many other miracles. **Up to the present time the Christian sect — so-called after him — has not ceased to exist.**"[51]

Many classical scholars look upon this passage as added by another hand at a later date.

....

50   Some may disagree with Brodrick's estimation of the Gospels as trusted historical data, but time and time again, they have been proven to be trustworthy in what they recorded. Even agnostic Bart Ehrman concedes the following points: "The Gospels certainly do contain historically important information about Jesus, especially when it comes to the very broad outlines of what he said, did, and experienced. With respect to the death of Jesus, for example, there are very good reasons indeed for being relatively certain that Jesus went from his home country of Galilee to the city of Jerusalem the last week of his life in order to celebrate the Passover meal; that there he aroused the anger of the Jewish leaders and Roman authorities; he was arrested, put on trial by the Roman governor Pontius Pilate; found to be guilty of treason against the state; and crucified. That basic story is reported in all the Gospels, and I think it is almost certainly right." In an interview with website, The Best Schools. https://thebestschools.org/special/ehrman-licona-dialogue-reliability-new-testament/ehrman-major-statement/
51   *Antiq. jud.*, xviii. cap. iv. The continued existence and success of the Christian church is one of the strongest evidences for the truth of the miraculous life of Jesus.

Tacitus is very explicit: "In order to quiet the report,[52] Nero accused and punished with the most refined tortures, those who with perverse obstinacy called themselves Christians. The Author of this name was Christ, who, during the reign of Tiberius, was executed by the Procurator Pontius Pilate."[53]

PURPOSE OF CHRIST'S MINISTRY

To understand the causes which led up to the arrest of Jesus Christ, we must look at the history of His three years' ministry. During that time He had lived, so to say, in the sight of all men, and under the scrutiny of a people who are and always have been intensely critical of their teachers. He had passed up and down the land from Galilee to Judaea, leading as everyone knew a life of poverty and the sternest asceticism and self-denial; ofttimes, as He Himself tells us, not knowing where to lay His head.

He had publicly healed the sick and cleansed the lepers, opened the eyes of the blind, and unstopped the ears of the deaf; He had made "the lame man to leap as a deer and the tongue of the dumb to sing."[54] He had fed the hungry and calmed the storm, had cured the epileptic, and blessed the little children, had bidden the evil demons that possessed a man body and soul begone and leave him, and He had on three occasions raised to life those who were physically dead. Nay more, He had gone further, and had preached repentance and the coming of the Kingdom of God amongst humanity. He had even forgiven the sins of the penitent in heart and of the diseased in body, and had sent them away with words of encouragement and hope; commanding them to lead a new life, and assuring them that, in spite of the severity of priests and Pharisees, He would not condemn them, for that He had not come "to break the bruised reed, nor quench the smoking flax."[55] These gracious deeds were not done to His fellow-countrymen and to people of His own faith alone, but also to Greek and Samaritan, the lost sheep of the House of Israel, and the Roman centurion.

....

52 Caused by the great fire in Rome.
53 *Ann.*, xv. 44.
54 Isaiah 35:6
55 Isaiah 42:3

He had taught incessantly during those three—openly in the Temple, in the local synagogues, on the hillside, and in a boat on the lake of Gennesaret—in fact anywhere and everywhere where men would listen to His teaching. In private also had He spoken deeply and earnestly to Martha and Mary at Bethany, and to Nicodemus in the midnight hour. **All acknowledged as they heard Him that "never has a man spoken as this Man,"[56] for "He taught with authority and not as the scribes."[57]** His message was eminently fitted to the comprehension of all sorts and conditions of men, from the learned master in Israel, to the ignorant Roman malefactor dying beside him.

Everyone who heard Him had been struck with the gracious words which proceeded out of His mouth, very different indeed from the dogmatism of the scribes, Pharisees, and lawyers, who insisted upon the strictest keeping of the letter of the law, the spirit of which they frequently evaded,[58] and while lading men with burdens grievous to be borne, touched not those burdens with one of their fingers.[59]

CENSURE OF PHARISEES AND SADDUCEES

He spoke not only smooth words to the people. His utterances were at times charged with fiercest denunciation against those who persisted in walking in hypocrisy and deceit. He fearlessly and with unflinching courage hurled winged words of fiery indignation and scathing sarcasm upon Pharisees and Sadducees, priests, and lawyers. He attacked them, not because they were powers in high places, but because being called upon by birth, by education, and by knowledge, to responsible and public positions in Israel, they were abusing, instead of using, their powers. They knew what was right, and deliberately chose the wrong. He unhesitatingly denounced them as hypocrites, blind guides, serpents, and the "offspring of vipers"[60]; as white-washed tombs

....

56   John 7:46
57   Matthew 7:29
58   Matt. 15:3-15, 23:3; Mark 7:5-9; Luke 11:42-45
59   Matt. 23: 23-33 ; Luke 11:39-52
60   Matt. 5:20 ; 13: 3-34 ; 15:3-15 ; 22:18

full of uncleanness. He bade his followers beware of the leaven, of the Pharisees, the Sadducees, and the Herodians,[61] namely their teaching, their example, and their life. He accused them of compassing sea and land to make one proselyte, and when they had secured him they made him twofold more the child of Gehenna than they were themselves,[62] and He boldly flung it at them that they should not escape the judgment of Gehenna.

He openly brought against them that most terrible of all accusations, that they hid the key of knowledge,[63] and that while not entering into the Kingdom themselves they prevented from going in many who fain would do so.[64] Finally, with the shadows of suffering and death hanging over Him, He poured forth the vials of his wrath upon them all collectively, and told them that they were of their father the devil, and his lusts they would do; consequently if they continued to work his works they should die in their sins;[65] and then as if to reassure them, He sarcastically observed that they need not be afraid that *He* would accuse them to the Father, that Moses on whom they set their hopes would do that, and that into the Kingdom of God, out of which they were thrusting many, the publicans and the harlots should enter before them.[66]

Can you wonder that they hated Him?

For His words must have stung their guilty consciences like red-hot arrows; and are you surprised that at last they felt they could bear it no longer, and sought for some means of stopping the preaching of the Prophet of Nazareth?

The scribes and Pharisees, the bulk of whom at this period were religious hypocrites, disliked Him; the Sadducees and Herodians —who were political opportunists—were bitterly antagonistic to Him. These latter, who thought only of keeping friends with the

....

61   Matt. 16:6 ; Mark 8:15 ; Luke 7:1
62   Matt. 23:15
63   Matt. 23:13
64   Luke 11:57
65   John 8:15-35
66   Matt. 21:31

Roman power, hated any idea of reformation, and were seized with a panic at any suggestion of revolution or even of tumult, so they were alarmed at possible consequences.

REFORMATION NOT REVOLUTION

And it was reform that the Master ceaselessly and untiringly inculcated—Reform not Revolution, Fulfilment not Destruction. It was not the abrogation [canceling] of the law, but the *keeping* of the law that Christ insisted upon, while at the same time He showed His co-religionists that the blind following of the letter was not sufficient, and that they could even transgress the spirit of the Divine Law by tying themselves down too rigidly to the dead traditions of the elders.

For Himself, He had — as a pious Jew — fulfilled all the requirements of the Mosaic code. He had been circumcised on the eighth day, and duly presented in the Temple; He went up to Jerusalem for the Passover and other Jewish feasts; and He was baptized by John at the beginning of His ministry 'for it becomes us to fulfill all righteousness.' Moreover, He required his disciples also to keep the observances of the Levitical law, and sent the healed leper to show himself to the priest and make the required offering. As a good citizen, He paid the half-shekel demanded by the Roman Procurator from everyone over twenty years of age, and bade his disciples render to Caesar his due. He gave them object lessons also on the keeping of the spirit of the Law times without end, as, when on the Sabbath Day he healed the man with the dropsy, released the woman "whom Satan had kept bound for eighteen years,"[67] and cured the man too old and too feeble to get by himself into the healing waters of Bethesda.

One asks the question: was it only because Christ spoke so openly, continuously, and uncompromisingly against the hypocrisy and avarice of the rulers in Jewry that they all hated Him so bitterly? May we not find in the troubled history of the Jews at this period some political reason also for their persistent determination to bring about His death?

....

67   Luke 13:16

Renan, in his valuable *Histoire du Peuple d'Isra'el*, gives us a clue to the national feeling and temper in Palestine under the later high priests. In looking at the history of the Hebrews, we find that after centuries of pastoral life and patriarchal government, they suddenly burst into a stationary and national life, asking for and obtaining a king to rule over them. They were neither prepared for it nor was it in any respect suited to their racial characteristics. The chieftain's tent and the movable ark were far more in accordance with their temperament and instincts than Solomon's Palace and the Temple at Jerusalem. There was never really any national ideal among the Jews. Very conservative, very superstitious, and very prejudiced, they were originally polytheists, then became nominally monotheists with Jehovah recognized as their one official deity, yet until the days of the exile they clung to their Teraphim [idols] and their Ephods [priestly garment], their Mazzêbahs [sacred pillars] and their Ashêrahs [images]. Few were the years that saw a king over an undivided people; and few and troublous were the centuries that saw first the division into two parts, and then the final break-up of that short-lived kingdom. The sad period of the Exile and Captivity followed, and when Judah once more returned to the land of their fathers it was to a kingless country and a ruined Temple.

Then arose the sway of the high priests, and nominally a theocratic government; and while the nation, busy in rebuilding the Temple and re-arranging the law never consolidated itself, the world around was arming for conquest. We all know the miserable story of Palestine under Seleucids and Romans, with its one bright page of Hasmonaean courage and devotion, then the curtain comes down on independent national life, and the country becomes nothing but a territory of Rome and the inhabitants thereof no longer a free people.

Primarily the Exile embittered the Jews, and after their return to their own land, the siding of the aristocratic classes with the Roman rulers, and the avarice and hypocrisy of the priests and Pharisees filled the loyal Jews — who were the masses — with indignation and disgust. Can you wonder that when a Prophet arose, preaching regeneration and reform, both religious and social, that "the common people heard him gladly,"[68] and hopes arose of the advent at no distant day of the Messiah — the Deliverer — the King? The whole nation was strung up at this time into such a state of tension that the slightest event was sufficient to produce political riot, or religious tumult; and on many occasions it was only the firm hand of the Roman Procurator and the close proximity of six thousand soldiers, that saved Jerusalem from revolutionary outbursts.

This new teaching had stirred up all Jewry so much so that a party composed of scribes and Pharisees actually went down from Jerusalem to Galilee, to interview the Prophet, and stop the propaganda — if possible — from spreading further. This was no easy matter, for He had the ear of the people. The whole nation was on the tiptoe of expectation, looking for the Deliverer. Over and over again in the four Gospels do we find this to be the case. At the baptism of Christ, "as all the people were in expectation,"[69] John the Baptist had pointed Him out as the Anointed of whom he (John) was but the forerunner.[70] "Are you the One who was to come, or should we look for another?"[71] was the question put to Him in varied forms times and again, both by the disciples of the Baptist and by His own followers.

POPULAR EXPECTATION OF THE MESSIAH

His doctrines differed essentially from those of their priests and lawyers, and were so full of graciousness and love that they were compelled to acknowledge that here was no ordinary prophet, but "a new teaching."[72] Thus the Messianic hope found expression, and many of the Jews felt that this *must* be the Deliverer who should come to Zion. They admitted first, that "a great Prophet has risen up among us,"[73] and that God has visited His people; and

....

68   Mark 12:37
69   Luke 3:15
70   Luke 3:15; John 1:29-34
71   Matthew 11:3
72   Mark 1:27
73   Luke 7:16

then, as He became more widely seen and known of His fellow-countrymen, they acknowledged in a burst of enthusiasm that He was "the Son of David,"[74] "the holy one of God,"[75] "the Christ of God,"[76] and finally, "the King of Israel"[77]— the Messiah. But how little did the Hebrew nation grasp the true nature and office of the Messiah.

Their hearts' desire was for an earthly potentate [ruler] who should restore again the kingdom to Israel; a royal soldier who would release them from the yoke of Rome and lead them to victory; a king greater than Solomon: one who should make their nation higher than all that were in the earth, who would bring back the scattered ones from far and near, and rebuild Jerusalem where His throne should be established forever and men should "bless themselves in His name."[78] It was not until the populace at last began to realize that this was no part of Christ's mission that they—ever fickle and easily disappointed—began to be offended at Him, and murmurs arose that, after all, He was but the carpenter's son.

"His father and mother we know."[79]

"However, we know where this Man is from; but when the Christ comes, no one knows where He is from."[80]

"Can it be that the rulers indeed know that this is the Christ?"[81]

and so on. Thus already in the three short years of His ministry had the Master begun to see fulfilled His own words, that He came to cast fire upon the earth, and to bring not peace, but a sword.

....

74   Matthew 1:1
75   Mark 1:24
76   Matthew 16:16
77   John 12:13
78   Psalm 72:17
79   John 6:42
80   John 7:27
81   John 7:26

TWO OPPOSING FORCES

So we find that there arose against Him two powerful factions; on the one hand the priests and the Pharisees, and on the other the Sadducees, and to these must be added a body of His own countrymen who were almost more dangerous, because more uneducated and irresponsible. Swayed now this way, now that, like sedges in a breeze, neither the Sanhedrin on the one hand, nor the Teacher Himself on the other, could tell from day to day what their attitude might be. Today they would take Him by force and make Him a king, and tomorrow try to throw Him down headlong from the hill whereon their city was built. They would shout "Hosanna to the Son of David" today, and tomorrow take up stones to cast at Him.

Palestine was on the verge of a religious revolt, and any disturbance would at once bring down with severity the iron hand of Rome. The Jews, more than any other subject people, had been allowed greater freedom in the management of their own internal and municipal affairs and in the practice of their religion and ritual; so that anything like a breach of the peace or sedition, if known to the Procurator, would be likely to considerably curtail these privileges.

Therefore for the political welfare of the nation, the Teacher must be suppressed.

The authorities first tried coercion and decreed, that if "any man should confess that Jesus was the Christ he should be put out of the synagogue,"[82] nevertheless, some of the rulers did believe on Him, though secretly, for fear of the Pharisees,[83] and multitudes of the common people still heard Him gladly.

Next, accusations were launched against Him of such a nature that they amounted practically to that most hideous of all Jewish crimes, *Læsæ Majestatis Divinæ*, i.e., treason against the Deity,

....

82   John 9:22
83   John 12:42

which in the statutes of the Hebrew commonwealth assumed a significance that we can hardly realize. To the Jews, Jehovah was their personal and absolute ruler. Kings, judges, and high priests were not so much His earthly representatives, as merely those courtiers to whom He graciously permitted access to His presence chamber. They conveyed His word, which was law, to the people of Israel. Therefore in that commonwealth anything that savored of "perverting the people,"[84] or sorcery, or of playing the part of a false prophet, or of "destroying this place and changing the customs which Moses delivered unto us,"[85] or even the slightest attempt made to alter the divine system of the law came under the head of constructive treason, while to make one's self out to be the Son of God and equal to God, unless it could be proved, was blasphemy.

The punishment for treason against God, and for blasphemy, was death.

FIRST ATTEMPT ON THE LIFE OF CHRIST

Once during the early part of His ministry, the Pharisees had been so angry with Him for publicly in the synagogue and on the Sabbath day, healing the man with the withered hand, that they "took counsel against Him how they might destroy Him";[86] but He withdrew from them. Again, later, the rulers—presumably the Sanhedrin— deliberately planned how they might compass without failure the arrest of the Prophet of Nazareth. We read of this first attempt in John 7:32, when at the Feast of Tabernacles during the autumn of A.D. 28 (?), about six months before the Passover "the chief priests and Pharisees sent officers to take Him"[87] in the Temple courts where He was teaching, and where evidently a disturbance was being created. Some of His hearers said, "This is the Christ," others again scorned the idea, and "there was a division among them." The Temple officers (*hypēretēs*), evidently afraid of the temper of the populace, returned without

....

84   Luke 23:2
85   Acts 6:14
86   Matt. 12:14
87   John 7:32

Him saying, "Never has a man spoken like this Man," to be answered by the scornful remark of the Pharisees, "Are you also led astray? Have any of the rulers believed on Him or of the Pharisees? But this people which know not the law is accursed."[88] Whereupon Nicodemus made a bold appeal to the conscience of the Council, "Does our law judge any man before it first *hears from himself* and *knows* what he does?" His question contains two of the fundamental principles of Jewish law:

I. a. That in a criminal case every opportunity shall be given to the accused to speak for himself, and to advance any point he can in his own favor.

    b. That anything said by him during the trial shall never be used as evidence against him, or even as tending to prejudice his case.

    c. A criminal trial shall be opened always with the defense, and not with the accusation.

II. The witnesses themselves must arrest the prisoner, and formulate in public and upon solemn oath their reason for so doing.[89]

COURAGE AND ACUMEN OF NICODEMUS

This determined attack upon the *liberty* of Christ was thus foiled by the courage of that timid ruler of the Jews who first came to Him secretly in the dead of night. It was a masterly stroke on the part of Nicodemus, and that short sentence contains the pith of Jewish criminal procedure. In a few words he had summed up the whole digest of their criminal *corpus juris*, and no member of the Council could fail to acknowledge the cogency [logic] of that insistence upon justice.

Two attempts to take mob law into their own hands and put Him to death are now recorded against the populace. Speaking in the

....

88   John 7:47-48
89   Mishna, *De Syn.*, iv.

treasury of the Temple a little later on, Christ had openly told them that He knew they sought to kill Him (John 8:37) and rebuked them for not believing on Him (v. 40), adding that for those who kept His sayings there was no death (v. 51), as before Abraham was "I AM"(v. 58). Whereupon the people in a paroxysm [violent expression] of fury declared Him to be possessed by a demon (v. 48) and tried to stone Him. But He escaped.

Again, a little later on in the winter time, during the Feast of the Dedication which took place on *Kisleu* 25th, i.e., towards the middle of December, they tried again to take Him up for blasphemy.[90]

Some of the Jews urged Him to keep them no longer in suspense, but once and for all to declare Himself the Christ, if so He was. His reply was the claim, "I and My Father are one,"[91] which so enraged them that they attempted again to stone Him. Once more He escaped and went away into the desert country east of the Jordan, from whence He was only recalled by the illness and death of His friend Lazarus. His visit to the bereaved sisters brought him back to Bethany, a village within a stone's-throw of the Holy City, where His raising of Lazarus and the consequent excitement among the people seem to have brought matters to a climax.

THE ADVICE OF CAIAPHAS

A council of the Sanhedrin[92] (*synedrion*) was hastily called together, and it was resolved that this state of popular ferment must be put an end to "lest the Romans come and take away our place and nation." whereupon Caiaphas, the worldly wise Sadducee, the degenerate high priest and the friend of Pontius Pilate, cynically observed, "You know nothing at all; it is far wiser to take the life of this *one Man* who is the cause of all this trouble than that a tumult arise which will assuredly come to the ears of the Procurator, for then the Romans *will* come and take away our place and nation; better far to sacrifice one life than that the whole nation perish." Advice which appeared reasonable to his colleagues.

....

90   John 10:22-33
91   John 10:30
92   John 11:47

From that moment, Christ's doom was sealed. An order was issued that if anyone knew where He was, he was to say so that the arrest might immediately take place. Not only was He to be apprehended, but Lazarus also, through whose influence many were believing on Him.[93] So from that day forth "they took counsel how they might put Him to death"; but He withdrew Himself into the city of Ephraim in the near eastern desert, and there remained until six days before the Passover.

Failing to capture Him at once, and the Passover drawing nigh, which would undoubtedly bring many of His friends and disciples to Jerusalem, thus increasing their difficulties, the chief priests and scribes sent forth spies to watch Christ and endeavor to provoke Him to do or say something that might bring Him into the hands of the *Roman* governor. They selected for their purpose the crucial question as to whether being Jews it was needful for them to pay tribute to Caesar; but they were not able to take hold of His answer before the people, and were once more foiled.

Thus in unsuccessful plotting, not now against the *liberty*, but against the very *life* of Christ, the days preceding the Passover wore away. They were within two days of the Feast, and still the *Mesith* [a false prophet or perverter of the people] was not only at large, but openly teaching in the Temple. In despair another meeting was hastily called in the palace of the high priest, consisting of the chief priests, elders of the people and scribes,[94] when it was agreed that for fear of a popular rising during the Feast in favor of the Teacher, He must be arrested *secretly*, [with deceit], and at once put to death. All four Gospels[95] expressly state this, and it seems as if the difficulties in taking Him were great, for finally Judas, one of His own specially chosen apostles who knew intimately His movements and His habits, offered to betray Him to His murderers—and for what? A paltry thirty shekels of silver, the price of an adult slave.

....

93   John 12:10-11
94   Matt. 26:3, Mark 14:1, Luke 22:2
95   Matt. 26:4, Mark 14:1-2, Luke 22:2, John 11:5

THE LEGALITY OF THE MEETING

Now comes the question, was this meeting a properly convened legal meeting of the Council? Had the scribes, priests, and elders of the people the power to arrest Jesus Christ for an *anticipated verdict*?

The writer of the Fourth Gospel alone mentions the Council at which Caiaphas urged the necessity for Christ's death, and he uses the strictly technical term (*synedrion*) for it. On the other hand, not one of the Synoptists, who all three mention the gathering in Caiaphas' house—which is omitted by the writer of the Fourth Gospel—call it by any legal title. Yet this was the meeting that actually condemned Him to death before arrest. The careful omission of any technical name, and the fact of the meeting being in the high priest's house and not in "the sheds,"[96] nor in the chamber called *Gazith*, make it very doubtful if this was indeed a legally constituted meeting of the Sanhedrin, or High Court of Justice, which alone could issue an order of arrest and which required a bench of seventy-one judges to consign the prisoner to capital punishment. "A whole tribe or a false prophet or a high priest, if they have to be judged for a crime which may bring capital punishment need a court of seventy-one judges," says the Rabbi Simeon ben Gamaliel. And it was for leading people astray, for being in fact a *Mesith*—a false prophet—that Jesus Christ was apprehended.

THE ARREST

The Rulers of the Jews having obtained the cooperation of Judas Iscariot, supplied him with the means of arresting Jesus Christ.

a. A great multitude with swords and staves.[97]

b. A multitude with swords and staves from the chief priests and elders.[98]

c. A multitude and he that was called Judas.[99]

....

96   The Chanoth, which was a place within the bounds of the temple.
97   Matt. 26:47
98   Mark 14:43
99   Luke 22:47

d. A band of soldiers and officers from the chief priests and the Pharisees. *(speira kai hypēretēs).*[100]

It is only the Fourth Gospel which speaks of "the band" *(speira,* Vulgate *cohors),* and the "chief captain" *(chiliarchos,* Vulgate *tribunus.*[101])

Are we to infer, from the silence of the Synoptists and this one mention of the military, that Roman authority had been requisitioned? We read that Judas received them from the Jewish governors, who most certainly had no power of themselves to call in the aid of Roman soldiers to arrest a Man upon whom they were intending to pass sentence of death for an ecclesiastical offence, neither was it the business of the Tribune to accompany soldiers upon a police affair, neither does the word *speira* necessarily imply a Roman armed band, nor is *chiliarchos* always and exclusively used in the technical sense. Judging from the statements of the Synoptists, I cannot help thinking that the "band and chief captain" may be taken to imply the Temple police or guard *(hypēretēs)* recruited from the ranks of the Levites, with their commanding officer *(strategos).*

If you accept the terms *speira* and *chiliarchos* in their technical sense you are brought face to face with the ludicrous spectacle of a dignified Roman Tribune in all his war panoply [a complete suit of armor] at the head of a cohort of six hundred men,[102] helping the Temple police and a Jewish rabble to hunt by torchlight in a garden for an unarmed and unresisting man.

It is too incredible.

Besides, the very last thing desired by the Sadducean element would be that at the Passover time, any idea of a tumult in Jerusalem should come to Roman ears. St. Peter's unwise and impulsive act would have at once resulted in his being bound and carried off a prisoner had the "band and chief captain" been Roman officials, for punishment speedily followed resistance to Imperial Rome.

....

100   John 18:3
101   John 18:12
102   A Roman cohort consisted of three maniples each containing two hundred men — or of six centuries, each century consisting of one hundred men.

THE TEMPLE GUARD

In all probability, "the band" sent to arrest Christ were the *shōterīm*, officials of the same nature as those who were sent to arrest Him during the Feast of Tabernacles.[103] Probably also they were the same force as that which was employed with "the captain— *strategos*—of the Temple" in apprehending Peter and John.[104]

St. Mark uses the word *speira*[105] when after the trial was over, the soldiers (*stratiōtēs*) led Him away into the Prætorium and called together the whole band (*speira*, Latin *cohors*). The *stratiōtēs* were undoubtedly the Roman soldiers, who are not mentioned by St. Mark as having been at the arrest. It does not seem probable that six-hundred of them, with their *chiliarchos* (Latin *tribunus*) would have been on guard in the palace at that early hour in the morning, nor that they would have been simultaneously called together to torment a helpless prisoner.[106] It is evident that the "whole band" was already on the spot, which points to the Jewish Temple guard (*shōterīm*) who until now had been responsible for the custody of the Prisoner.

Had the arrest of Jesus Christ been ordered by the permission of the Procurator and with the aid of Roman soldiers, there is not the slightest doubt but that He would have been put in custody in the castle of Antonia until the next day, and then brought straight before Pilate.[107]

THE ILLEGALITY OF THE ARREST

Two questions now confront us:

    1. Was the arrest of Jesus Christ legally carried out?

    2. Had the Sanhedrin of that day the right to arrest him?

....

103   John 7:32-45
104   Acts 4:1, 4:22-26
105   Mark 15:16
106   Mark 15:17-20
107   See A. Loisy, *Le IVme Évangile* who draws the same conclusion from a totally different line of argument.

In connection with the first question, the Mishna lays down the following regulations:

a. Arrest before trial was not permitted unless it was practically certain that either escape or armed resistance was contemplated.

b. Arrest after sunset was illegal.

c. It was not lawful to bear arms at the Passover time.

d. The witnesses themselves must arrest the accused and bring him before the court.

e. Arrest upon a count that was likely to end in sentence of death was not permitted at Passover time.

f. It was illegal to arrest any man for a predetermined conviction.

Every one of these regulations was violated.

Jesus Christ was arrested for the express purpose of being put to death, during the night of the 14 or 15 Nisan which was the Passover time, not by the witnesses who would later on be His public accusers, but by a band of armed men to whom He was betrayed by a renegade friend. He was arrested by order of the Sanhedrin, not as a preventive measure, but as an executive act.

The second question is more difficult to answer, as the jurists themselves are by no means all of one mind upon the subject; and we shall have to discuss it later on. Castelli[108] and several other writers maintain that with the conquest of Judaea by Rome, there passed away not only the right of the Jewish court to *try* capital cases, but even to *arrest* the criminal.

On the other hand, Salvador and Mommsen emphatically declare that the Sanhedrin had still the right both of arrest and trial for capital crimes, and could even condemn the prisoner to death, but that they could no longer carry the execution into effect; Rome as the conqueror reserving this right *always* to herself.

....

108   *Legge del popolo Ebreo*, cap. viii.

At any rate I think it is quite clear that the Sanhedrin were within their privileges, if not their rights, in *permitting* the arrest of Jesus Christ, as He was accused of purely ecclesiastical offenses, and none that in any way touched or even remotely concerned Roman laws. But, as a judicial body, they had no power to arrest Him. It was the duty of the witnesses who would subsequently be His accusers in open court to do this, though the Sanhedrin might facilitate matters by granting the help of the Temple police.

Having apprehended their Prisoner, the legal duty of the band was to guard Him securely until the Sanhedrin was next in session; which, being the eve of the Passover, would not have been until after the Feast, the Octave, and the following Sabbath were over, thus postponing the trial for nine days.[109]

Instead of doing this they took Him bound to the palace of the ex-high priest Annas alone — for all His disciples had fled — but followed ultimately by that one, who, knowing the high priest, went in with the officers. He was thus in all probability the only disciple present at the interrogation by Annas and the trial before Caiaphas. The Synoptists, not being on the spot, have only recorded what took place from hearsay, and this may account for their omission to mention the disciple's presence in the court and his obtaining permission for Peter to enter. St. Mark, who probably gives St. Peter's account of the events of that night, states that Peter remained below in the court with the servants.[110]

The absence of the other disciples will also help to explain the obvious discrepancies and variations contained in the accounts of what took place on that fateful night. We are bound to consider them carefully; but they do not any of them present insuperable difficulties. They are only such as we might expect to find in four separate accounts of the same events written by four different people at various intervals of time after those events took place, and in three instances by men who were not eyewitnesses. Fortunately, the most hopeless discrepancy for us to reconcile (the exact date of the arrest, trial, and crucifixion)

....

109   Mishna, *Moed Katon*, xi. 2.
110   Mark 14:66

in no way affects any legal question, and we are therefore not called upon to discuss it.

To follow the exact sequence of events is a matter of difficulty. St. John alone records the interrogation by Annas,[111] St. Luke alone mentions the transfer to Herod,[112] while Matthew and Mark relate that He was taken by night to the palace of Caiaphas and there interrogated by the Council, who produced false witnesses to bear testimony against Him. These two latter Evangelists also state that in the morning another consultation took place, apparently still in the high priest's house, but perhaps before a larger number of the chief priests, scribes, and elders.[113] St. Luke again differs from them all, by stating simply "that they brought Him into the high priest's house," and he records no trial before Caiaphas. His account reads as if our Lord had merely been detained and tormented by the guard until dawn, when He was led away into the Council Hall of the Sanhedrin, from where He was taken to Pilate.[114]

St. Matthew alone mentions the dream of Pilate's wife, and the washing of the governor's hands.[115]

PECULIARITIES OF JEWISH LAW

We come now to the record of those events in our Lord's trial, which are in direct conflict with Hebrew law and procedure, and concerning which much has been written by both Jewish and Christian writers. The fact that the latter invariably approach the question from a Christian standpoint, with a veil of Roman law and modern usage before their eyes, invalidates much that they have said upon the subject. On the Mishna itself must lie the onus of proving illegality and injustice.

Jewish legislature was essentially Oriental, peculiar entirely to itself, and cannot be compared with any modern, western code.

....

111   John 18:13
112   Luke 23:7
113   Matt. 27:1, Mark 15:1
114   Luke 22:54, 23:1
115   Matt. 27:19-24

It was made for a theocratic commonwealth of pastoral people, in which the life of each individual was most carefully guarded.

Roman law had its foundation in a western, military system controlled by the Imperator, who was at once commander-in-chief, high priest, and chief judge.

Christian lawyers who have written upon the subject have invariably annulled the value of their writings, by endeavoring to prove that the Sanhedrin had no *legal* right to do this or that or the other, because it was not the course which they consider legal, and quote the principles of Roman law to back up their *dicta*. A method which seems to be wholly wanting in common-sense.

To understand Hebrew law and its methods, we must consult those learned Jewish rabbis and lawyers who have given their time and attention to elucidating [clarifying] and explaining their own legal code. Foremost among modern jurists stands Salvador, a learned Spanish Jew, whose history of the Mosaic institutions is a European classic, and who devoted years to the study and exposition of the Talmud.

Maimonides, Mommsen, and Rabbinowicz among many others have written learnedly and thoughtfully upon the same subject. Therefore, by following the Mishna itself and the aforesaid scholars' commentaries upon it, we are more likely to obtain a right view of the complicated questions that will confront us.

Would you go to a [Muslim] *ulema* to ask for an explanation of Christian doctrine? Then why consult a modern European and Christian lawyer upon questions of ancient and Jewish law? The last book of any importance that has been written upon the subject and which created some stir on its publication, was Rosadi's *Il processo di Gesù*, the work of a brilliant Tuscan advocate; but it is inaccurate and misleading, chiefly because — misstatements apart (of which there are many) — he applies ancient Roman law as exemplified in modern Italian procedure to a Jewish trial that took place nineteen hundred years ago. Where the two different legal systems do not coincide, he emphatically denounces the Sanhedrin as in the wrong, denying them even the right to try an ecclesiastical offender. Undoubtedly the rulers of the Jews conducted the trial with serious forms of illegality; but the Mishna and not the Pandects of Justinian, must show cause where justice was not done, and murder committed.

THE TALMUD

We will now turn to the Talmud, that "encyclopedia of all law," as it has been called, and see by what legal process the Council had power thus arbitrarily to order the arrest of the Teacher, having already prejudged and condemned Him.

The word *Talmud* means literally a teaching, an inference, or a doctrine. It is a collection of works embodying the oral law of the Hebrews. The Jews declare that "Moses received Torah — or Law — (which includes the Pentateuch and the oral teaching) from Sinai, delivered it to Joshua, Joshua to the elders, and the elders to the prophets. The prophets delivered it to the men of the Great Synagogue; these last being the most important teachers, of whom a list of pairs is given reaching down to Hillel and Shammai, who lived in the early days of Christ."[116] It was supposed to be based upon the *Shema* or Jewish profession of faith that was recited twice daily by every pious Jew. As time went on it gradually became orally expanded into such a vast compilation of legal enactments and quibbles, traditions and usages, discussions and decisions, commentaries and illustrations, that at last it was absolutely chaotic; all the more so that it was looked upon as a religious offense to codify it in writing. It contains many other things besides law, but out of the forty volumes of the Talmud, by far the oldest are the twelve volumes of law, pure and simple, called the Mishna, i.e., the Repetition. "The Mishna is divided into six sections termed *Sedarim*. Each *Seder* is divided into *Masechtoth* or treatises. Each *Masechta* is again subdivided into chapters called *Perakim*. The Masechta entitled 'Sanhedrin' is the fourth treatise of the Seder or section termed *Nezikin*, or damages which embraces a great part of the civil and criminal law."[117]

....

116   Mishna, *Pirké Avoth*, i. b.
117   Mielziner

In particular, it gives the scope and composition of the Sanhedrin — the Jewish High Court of Justice — the methods of procedure in trials, and the laws concerning the examination of witnesses, capital punishment, and "forty stripes save one." It decrees how oaths — both those taken in private and openly in court — are to be administered, and it defines the law of evidences.

This legal code which professed to be based upon the Mosaic law began, as a matter of fact, to supersede it after the return from the captivity and the establishment of local synagogues. During the period of the Second Temple, it was continually enlarged; commentaries were made upon it, and commentaries again upon those commentaries until about the second century A.D., when the original law bade fair to be entirely lost in minute and detailed dissertations. Thus, from the days of the return from Babylon this oral law had been gradually accumulating, and the trend of the Mishna in each succeeding generation had been to multiply precautions against any possibility of injustice towards, or negligence of, the interests of the prisoner. Its great object was to ensure for every one, however lowly his station, full publicity in any trial which might end in capital punishment.[118] In this respect one might almost describe Jewish law as extremely cautious. "Be cautious and slow in judgment, raise up many disciples, and make a fence round the law," was a favorite axiom of the rabbis.

THE WORK OF THE RABBIS

The learned Hillel, who presided over the Sanhedrin during the reign of Herod the Great, was the first who attempted to reduce this legal chaos to order, and arranged the Mishna into six divisions. Then followed in the second century, A.D., the rabbi Akiba, who took out all the subject matter of those six divisions, arranging them under their correct headings, and tabulating them. The rabbi Meir, a disciple of Akiba, continued his master's work, and may be said to have finally arranged the law. In the beginning of the third century, A.D., came the Rabbi Jehuda Hannasi, a very wealthy and learned Jew of irreproachable life, and a great friend of the Roman authorities. He was the head of one of the Palestinian Academies

---

118   Mishna, *Cap. Patrum*, i. b.

founded for the express purpose of studying and handing down legal tradition, and with a band of devoted disciples gave up his time and wealth to codifying and setting down the oral law in writing. Many of his opinions were based upon those of his great predecessors — Hillel and the two Gamaliel's.

In the century immediately before Christ, schools were established under *Tannaim* or teachers, for the express purpose of explaining the law, and instructing children in it. Although the Mishna had not been reduced to writing at the time of Christ's trial, Jewish writers generally concur in admitting that the criminal code there enunciated was the same as that in use in the days of Caiaphas.

The Jewish Church considered the Law to be more inspired than the rest of their sacred books, and a vast amount of time was spent in trying to squeeze cryptic and allegorical meanings out of even the plainest directions, these being applied equally to the greatest emergencies or the most trifling details of everyday life. Thus, at the date when Christ was brought to trial for perverting the nation, the life of a Hebrew was so carefully hedged round, so marvelous and intricate were the precautions and the legal quibbles, so many gnats were strained out and so many camels swallowed whole, that capital punishment was almost an impossibility. The old rabbi Meir writes: "What doth God say — if one may speak after the manner of men of God — when the malefactor suffers the anguish of his crime? He says: 'My head and my limbs are pained'; and if He so speaks of the guilty, what must He utter when the righteous is condemned?"[119]

Eleazar, the son of Azarias, maintains that the Sanhedrin, which once in seventy years condemns a man to death, is a slaughter house;[120] and the two Rabbis, Akiba and Tarphon go even further, and declare that if only they were members of the Sanhedrin, no one should ever suffer the death sentence, to which sentiment Simeon, the son of Gamaliel retorts that, "such scholars would only increase bloodshed in Israel."[121]

....

119   Mishna, *De Syn*, vi. 5.
120   Ibid., *Makhoth*.
121   Ibid., *Makhoth Stripes*.

THE SANHEDRIN

The whole underlying principle of Jewish legal procedure at this period tended towards the multiplication of precautions against any possible miscarriage of justice. To carry these out effectually it was decreed that no one man should ever judge a cause: "Be not a sole judge; there is no sole judge but One."[122]

From Deut. 16:18-20, it is clear that as far back as pre-exilic days there was some organized method of judging the people with righteous judgment. It was probably carried out then by means of a Council of the heads of the tribes, which as time went on developed into the central and local Courts of Justice known as the great Sanhedrin and the minor Sanhedrins. These latter were established in towns of not less than one-hundred and twenty adult males, and were composed of twenty-three members, both priests and lay men, although in order to form a Sanhedrin the Council need not necessarily contain a priestly member.[123]

The Great Sanhedrin (*synedrion*) was "the highest Court of Justice and Supreme Council" in Jewry, and sat in Jerusalem itself. It received its Greek title in the second century, B.C., and was probably the descendant of the great assembly of the elders convened by Nehemiah and Ezra after the return from the captivity.[124]

It was entirely reconstituted after the fall of Jerusalem, first at Jamnia and then at Tiberias. This court was evidently looked upon by Christ, who speaks of it as judging capital offences,[125] as *the* supreme tribunal in His day.

Two maxims were supposed to regulate the deliberation of its judges:

      1. Thou shalt do no unrighteousness in judgment.

      2. Be cautious and slow in judgment.

....

122   Ibid., *Pirké Avoth*, iv. 8.
123   *De Syn*, i. par 6; x. par 2. Mommsen's *Les prov. Rom.*, xi. 479-503.
124   Nehemiah 8:10
125   Matt. 5:21

The members were called Elders, and are often alluded to in the Gospels; and in Christ's time these Elders were chiefly recruited from the ranks of the Sadducees. There were various methods of election to the Great Sanhedrin prevailing at different periods of history; but at that with which we are dealing any Jew who was well versed in Law and Tradition, and had publicly distinguished himself as a judge in his own locality, might become first a member of one of the two lesser Synedria in Jerusalem, afterwards rising to be an elder of the Great Sanhedrin, which was the highest dignity a judge could attain.[126] Besides legal ability, the personal qualifications that were theoretically required were so exacting that it is incredulous]that any human being was found worthy to sit in that magic semicircle.

In order to be elected, the candidate must be a man of good birth; tall, strong, and in good health; married, and the father of a family. He must be venerable, though not too advanced in years, dignified in bearing, and of good courage. He was required to be deeply learned, yet modest withal, able to speak in foreign tongues (Aramaic, Greek, and Latin), and he must have been initiated into the mysteries of Egyptian magic. It was also necessary that he should be held in good repute by his fellow men, and be wealthy besides, so as to be above suspicion of taking bribes. Any man who was blind, a dice player, or a fowler [one who snares birds], was not eligible for office.

This legal senate consisted of seventy-one judges. To assist them in their labors and adjudicate in minor causes were two courts, each one composed of twenty-three judges, known as the Lesser Sanhedrins. Presiding over the Great Sanhedrin was "the Father of the House of Justice,"[127] the high priest being only an *ex-officio* President, except in ecclesiastical cases when he was *de facto* President.[128] This accounts for the prominent part taken by Caiaphas at our Lord's trial, as in His time Hillel and Simon his son were respectively President and Vice-President, though there are some scholars who think that Gamaliel I, the son of Simon ben

---

126   José ben Chalaftha; Tosefta, *Shekalim*
127   *Yoma*, vii. 5.
128   Tosefta, *Pesachim*, iv.

Hillel, and the teacher of Saul of Tarsus, was President at that date.

COMPOSITION OF THE COURT

Apparently, the number of judges required to form a full court differed according to the gravity of the crime;[129] for we read: "To decide upon the following cases three persons are needed— civil cases, robbery, wounds, damages, and half damages. The same number are also required in the case of libel," etc. (Deut. 22:19); though some of the Talmudists declare that for libel twenty-three are needed, as libel might entail capital punishment.

"A whole tribe, or *a false prophet*, or a high priest, if they have to be judged for a crime which may bring capital punishment, shall be judged by a court of seventy-one judges, of whom there must never be fewer than twenty-three on the bench during the whole trial. If any man require to go out in order to do his business, let him look round to see if his colleagues be twenty-three. If they be, let him go; if not, let him wait until another enter in."[130]

The Mishna gives us the reason for these particular numbers:

- "From where do we deduce that the Great Sanhedrin must be seventy-one?"
  - "From 'Gather unto me seventy men' (Numbers 11:16), and add Moses, who was the head of them— hence seventy-one."
- "And from where do we deduce that a small Sanhedrin must be twenty-three?"
  - "From 'the congregation shall judge' and 'the congregation shall save,'"[131] we see that one congregation judges and the other congregation saves—hence there are twenty, as a congregation consists of not less than ten personages.

....

129   In matters concerning the composition and functions of the Sanhedrin, José ben Chalaftha, a well-known and learned Jewish historical writer and Talmudist, is safer to follow than Josephus.

130   Mishna, *De Syn*, i.; Lightfoot, *Hor. Heb.*, ii. 462.

131   Numbers 35:24-25

- "From where do we deduce that three more are needed?"
  - o "From 'Thou shalt not follow a multitude to do evil'";[132] from which we may infer that thou shalt follow them to do well.
  - o "But if so, why is it written at the end of the same verse: 'Incline after the majority to wrest judgment?'"
    - ▪ "This means that the inclination to free the man must not be similar to the influence to condemn; as to condemn, a majority of two is needed, while to free, a majority of one suffices. And a court must not consist of an even number, as if their opinion is halved no verdict can be established; therefore, one more must be added. Hence it is twenty-three."[133]

A certain number of students were attached to the Sanhedrin courts for the purpose of acquiring knowledge of law and procedure. Two scribes, doctors of the law, sat at a table to record the proceedings and sentence, and two officers — members of the Temple police called *shōterīm* — guarded the prisoner in court.[134]

TIME OF SESSION

According to José ben Chalaftha, "the judges sat from the offering of the morning until the offering of the evening sacrifice; but not on the Sabbath day, nor on feast days, nor in the Passover week." When in court they arranged themselves in a half circle, so that each man's face was visible to all his colleagues. In the center was the President, with the Vice-President and the High Priest on either hand; the rest of the Council were placed in the order of their seniority, the youngest members being at the outsides. Judgment usually went by the voting of the members. "In questions of civil law and in those affecting ecclesiastical and ceremonial law, the taking of the vote began with the principal

132 Exodus 23:2
133 Mishna, *De Syn*, cap. i.
134 *De Syn.*, iii.; Maimonides, *De Syn.*,i. 3; Haghighà, 16.

member of the Sanhedrin; in judgments of life and death, at the side — the younger ones thus voting first so as not to be influenced in any degree by their seniors."[135]

From the Great Sanhedrin in Jerusalem "went forth direction for all Israel," and their decisions were binding upon all other *synedria*, doctors, and teachers. It was the Jewish High Court of Appeal as well, and it was the only law court competent to judge certain cases — eight in number.[136]

The judges assembled in the *Lishcath ha Gazith*, or Hall of Hewn Stones, within the Temple area, situated on the south side. The Lesser Sanhedrins sat respectively in the "entrance to the Temple mount," and the "entrance of the Temple court."[137]

When under the first Roman governor the Jewish nation was deprived of the power of carrying out the death sentence, the sessions were removed to "the Sheds," or "Bazârs of the sons of Annas," which were in an outer court of the Temple, and were probably part of the market where people bought and sold doves, and the moneychangers set up their tables. "Forty years before the Temple was destroyed, judgment in capital cases was taken away from Israel, and the Council removed, and sat in the sheds."[138]

The Sanhedrin of Christ's day, apart from the purely priestly members, included Pharisees, Sadducees, and scribes — three factions with distinctly conflicting interests.

THE PHARISEES

The Pharisees, i.e., "the separated ones," became a distinctive set in the second century, B.C., when in the days of Antiochus Epiphanes there arose a strong Hellenizing party in Palestine, Simon, a "guardian" of the Temple, giving Onias III, the high

....

135   *De Syn.*, iv. 2; Tosefta, *San*, vii. 2.
136   *De Syn.*, i. 5.
137   *De Syn.*, i. 6; Middoth, v. 2.
138   Babylonian Talmud, *Aboda Zara*, 8 b, f 8.

priest, much trouble on this score.[139]

This movement spread rapidly among the priestly aristocracy, and even many of the lower orders, both of priests and people, appear to have joined it. To combat this national danger the Hasidean party was formed, who resolved to leave no stone unturned to enforce in its utmost strictness every jot and tittle of the law. The Hasideans and the Hellenizers soon came into opposition, and may thus be said to be, in a sense, the precursors of the Pharisees and Sadducees. The one set being distinctly a religious sect, the other a political party; although when the Jews lost their national independence the Sadducees naturally became less political, and came to be looked upon more in the light of a religious body.

Being religious and not political, the Pharisees survived the destruction of Jerusalem, when their leaders under the rabbi Hillel settled down first at Jamnia and then at Tiberias. Separating themselves as much as they could from all interaction with either Gentiles or Christians, and enforcing more rigorously than ever the letter of the law, they became at last a sect of Judaic priests and fanatics, whose lives were one long spiritual slavery. In Christ's day they were partly a legal, partly a religious body, holding vehemently "the tradition of the elders," and were both narrow-minded and hypocritical. They were, in fact, at that time, the Puritans of the Jewish Church. Josephus says that they taught the doctrine of the immortality of the soul, and believed future rewards and punishments to be consequent upon earthly conduct. He also states that they averred [asserted] that some things in life were the result of "Fate," and impossible to control, while with regard to other matters, man had the power of choosing what he would or would not do. Theirs was, in fact, a convenient doctrine of limited Free Will. They, with their strict observance of the Levitical law, came early into collision with Christ.

According to their views, He was undermining that which they spent their whole lives in trying to enforce, and was practically proclaiming that the greater number of their most dearly loved

139   Maccabees, iii; iv. 6.

regulations were unnecessary. They looked forward to the establishment of an ideal Jewish kingdom upon earth by one of the line of David, in which the Levitical law, as taught by them, should be kept in every little detail. Until that blessed time came, they must endure the chastening of the Lord in the shape of foreign rule, as a punishment for their sins.

It must also be remembered that they were always stirring up the populace against the Roman power. They refused to take the oath of allegiance to Caesar, and they haggled over paying the Imperial taxes.[140] Against Pharasaic formalism and tyranny, Christ strenuously set his face — pleading for justice, mercy, and the love of God, instead of the strict tithing of mint, annise [herb in the parsley family], and cumin [Eastern spice].

THE SADDUCEES

The Sadducees were the followers of the above-mentioned Hellenizers, and became a very strong political faction; so much so that in the time of Herod they formed the preponderating [majority] influence in the Sanhedrin, even the high priests for several generations being drawn from their ranks.

As a class they were enormously wealthy, and consequently very powerful. They were political aristocrats, in contrast to the Pharisees who were religious democrats, and who considered them very lax, not to say godless.

In B.C. 37, Herod put forty-five Sadducean members of the Sanhedrin to death on account of their outrageous lawlessness,[141] while he left the Pharisees untouched as they had great influence over the people, and also because at that moment, as there was no help for it, they had not openly opposed the Romans, arguing that they (the Romans) were Jehovah's curse upon the nation for their evil doings. Archelaus, Herod's successor, wisely left the municipal and religious affairs of Judaea in the hands of the Jews,

---

140 Josephus, *Antiq.*, x.; xv. 4.
141 Josephus, *Antiq.*, xvi. 2.

which meant that the power of the Sanhedrin became paramount on those questions, and consequently strengthened the influence of the Sadducees. It was, however, to the Pharisees in the Council that the people looked for religious direction, and as late as the reign of Agrippa I. They were offering the daily sacrifice, and practicing the Law.

When Jerusalem fell, the high priestly office passed away forever, and with the priesthood was swept away the Sadducean party.

The ideal of the Sadducees was to form a Jewish state in amity [friendship] with Rome, in which they might live comfortably, not to say luxuriously. They were thus diametrically [directly] opposed to the Pharisees, with whom they first came into collision in the reign of John Hyrcanus. In religious matters they declined to consider the oral law as *binding*, though they accepted the written law. They were very severe in carrying out the Lex Talionis [law of retaliation], and were harsh judges in the Sanhedrin trials, except in the matter of punishing false witnesses, in which the Pharisees were even sterner judges. Although numerically they formed a strong majority, they practically had no influence, either secular or religious, upon their compatriots.

Josephus says that the Sadducees denied the resurrection of the body, and thought the soul died with it, which belief, of course, includes the denial of future rewards and punishments. Acts 23:8 says they believed in neither angels nor spirits. They considered man to be absolutely a free agent and complete master of his own destiny, in contra-distinction to the Pharisees, who believed in a mixture of Fate, God, and Free Will. As Wellhausen has pointed out, they were entirely dependent upon their own resources; they claimed nothing from God, nor He from them.

Only at the end of Christ's ministry do we find them coming into direct collision with Him, when He interfered, as they considered, with their privileges, so they joined the Pharisees against him, and being friends of Pilate, tried to prove His disloyalty to Rome. Probably they formed a strong condemning party in the Sanhedrin, as they lived in a state of perpetual panic for fear of political consequences.

The writer of the fourth gospel never mentions them by name, although the term "chief priests" must of course include them.

THE SCRIBES

The scribes or *sōpherîm* of Christ's day were practically jurists, many of them were Pharisees, and none of them had any political influence. Their great ambition was to gain honor in the Temple and the synagogues, and admiration from their students.

Their chief functions were:
  a. To develop the law.
  b. To teach the law.
  c. "To act as judges in the Sanhedrin, and in the local courts."

Not only were they required to expound the Law and oral tradition, but they were expected also to spend time in imagining possible difficult cases which might arise, and arrange how they should be met. Thus, they overburdened themselves and their pupils with a mass of legal traditions, quibbles, and regulations, which called forth our Lord's sternest condemnation. Dr. Eaton has shown how they reduced piety to formalism, leaving no room for spontaneous devotion and warm-hearted religion. "Life under the Law was felt to be a heavy burden, and the scribes themselves had to devise methods whereby to evade some of their own precepts.[142] Instead of proving a help to men in their moral and religious life, the Law had become a means whereby access to God was cut off."[143]

In order to "raise up many disciples," their one endeavor was to gather round them as many of the Jewish youth as possible, propounding to them difficult and intricate legal quibbles, and disputing with them upon points of doctrine. The primary duty of the pupils was to train their memories to be retentive, never to teach anything other than what their masters had previously

....

142   Matt. 23:16; Luke 11:46
143   Luke 11:52

taught to them, and to "be quick to hear and slow to forget."[144]

Tradition was their fetish [obsession] — so much so that of Eliezer ben Hyrcanus it was said that he was "a plastered cistern that loses not a drop." The scribes were supposed to teach *gratis*, and make their living by other means than the Law, although there are many scholars who think that at this period they were paid; and there are passages in the Gospels which give weight to this opinion.[145]

"Whosoever makes profit from the words of Torah (Law) removes his life from this world."[146]

From the composition of the court, it seems unreasonable to think that the judges would try a *Mesith*, that is, a perverter or seductor of the people, or a case of blasphemy and sedition — especially where the element of personal dislike formed a strong factor — with strict impartiality and justice.

....

144   "He who teaches against the Pentateuch is not condemned to death, for all men know the Bible; but if he teaches anything against the doctors he is condemned." — Rabbinowicz, *Législation criminelle du Talmud.*
145   Matt. 10:10; Mark 12:40; Luke 10:7, 16:40, 20:47.
146   *Pirké Aboth,* iv. 9.

Lecture II:
The Trial and Condemnation

Topics Covered: Annas the High Priest, Caiaphas the High Priest, Probable Sequence of Events, The Questionable Legality of the Morning Sanhedrin Trial, The Importance of the Witnesses, Method of Criminal Procedure, Forms of Oral Evidence, Voting Procedure, The Punishment, The Question of Adherence to the Law, The Second Condemnation, The Definition of Blasphemy, The Power of the Sanhedrin, Pontius Pilate, The Verdict, The Condemnation, Pilate as Judge.

THE TRIAL AND CONDEMNATION

"When a judge decides not according to truth he makes the majesty of God to depart from Israel. But if he judges according to truth — were it only for one hour — it is as if he established the whole world, for it is in judgment that the Divine Presence in Israel has its habitation."[147]

Having secured their Victim the "officers from the chief priests and Pharisees," followed by Simon Peter and another disciple, recrossed the Wâdy Kidron, and ascending the steep pitch that led to the Temple enclosure, took Him straightway to Annas the ex-high priest, who was father-in-law to Caiaphas the high priest *de facto*.

ANNAS THE HIGH PRIEST

Annas ben Seth, the ninth high priest, dating from the reign of Herod, was appointed to that office in the year 7 A.D. by Quirinius. In the year 16 A.D., soon after the accession of the Emperor Tiberius, he was summarily deposed by the Procurator Valerius Gratus, the predecessor of Pontius Pilate, for exceeding the powers permitted to the Sanhedrin, and executing several Jewish prisoners without first obtaining a warrant from the Roman governor.

....
147   Taylor Innes, *Legal Monograph*

He was an enormously wealthy Sadducee, and having innumerable kinsmen in the Sanhedrin, besides five immediate relations who at one time or other held the Pontificate, was a personage exercising great influence in Jerusalem. He is said to have been a keen intriguer [one who schemes], and after his deposition, to have meddled considerably in affairs pertaining to the high priesthood.[148] Josephus says that not only did he manage to get five of his sons appointed high priests in succession, but that he also contrived to hold all the important and lucrative posts in the Temple itself. Certain it is that he and his family monopolized the sale of all the materials required for the offerings and sacrifices. These were allowed to be sold in the outer courts of the Temple itself, and on the Mount of Olives, and were known as the Booths of Annas. At the great feasts when all the countryside flocked to Jerusalem, an immense and extortionate trade was done in these necessary articles; hence our Lord's wrath at His Father's house being turned into a "house of merchandise"[149] and a "den of robbers."[150]

So intensely were Annas and his family hated that there is a curse against them in the Talmud — "Woe to the house of Annas, woe to their serpent hissings."[151]

Although he was no longer the actual high priest, he was still so *de jure*; **as arguing from Numbers 35:25-28, the Jews considered that a man once anointed as high priest — no matter what happened subsequently — remained a high priest forever. Probably they considered that Valerius Gratus had no right to depose Annas, and although they were obliged to acknowledge Caiaphas as the acting high priest, they did so under protest and continued to regard the former as their high priest still. This accounts for St. John calling Annas the high priest as well as Caiaphas,[152] and for St. Luke speaking of the combined high**

....

148   Josephus, *Antiq.*, x. 5; xx. 8.
149   John 2:16
150   Matthew 21:13
151   Pesahim 57a, *Talmud*
152   John 18:3

priesthood of Annas and Caiaphas.[153] In the Acts of the Apostles, Annas is distinctly spoken of as the high priest, which is the last time he is mentioned by name in the New Testament,[154] though he is alluded to on two other occasions.[155]

Annas, sitting alone at night, began to interrogate privately the Prisoner, and by asking Him two leading questions, endeavored first to make Him incriminate His disciples, and then incriminate Himself out of His own mouth.[156]

To the first question our Lord vouchsafed no reply — it was too utterly ungenerous.

To the second He gave an answer, appealing at the same time to the fundamental principle of Hebrew law. "I have spoken without reserve in Temple and synagogue, and in secret have I said nothing. Why do you ask *Me*? Ask those *who heard Me*."[157] This was a reminder to Annas, an elder of the Sanhedrin and therefore a jurist, that the question should have been addressed to the witnesses and not to the prisoner. It was the voice of the Hebrew citizen claiming justice and the right of fair trial from his interrogator who knew well enough that in questioning his solitary prisoner privately and in the dead of night, he was himself committing a serious breach of that very law he was in duty bound to administer justly. This plea was unanswerable; the ex-high priest was silent. After the insulting blow dealt by one of the bystanders, Christ again took his stand upon his rights and insisted upon the evidence of the witnesses. "If I have done evil, *bear witness* of the evil."[158]

Probably we in Europe in this twentieth-century[159] hardly realize the extraordinary importance of the witnesses in an ancient Jewish 'trial for life.' The prisoner could not even be legally arrested except by them; not only must the initiative come from them,

....

153   Luke 3:2
154   Acts 4:6
155   Acts 7:1, 9:1
156   John 18:19
157   John 18:20-21
158   John 18:23
159   Remember, Mary is writing in England in 1908!

but the whole onus and responsibility of the trial rested upon the witnesses alone. Nothing, in fact, could be legally carried out without them.

In their absence Jesus Christ was an unaccused man. Annas could do nothing.

Now this interrogation of our Lord by Annas was flagrantly illegal from another point of view also. It was forbidden under any circumstances to question a suspected man in private before he was formally brought to public trial by the witnesses, of whom there must be at least two. No personal investigations were allowed.

Upon this point Salvador is very definite: '*Un principe perpétuellement reproduit dans les écritures hébraïques, résume déjà les deux conditions de publicité et de liberté. On ne soumettait pas l'homme accusé à des interrogatoires occultes, où dans son trouble l'innocent peut fournir des armes mortelles contreclui.*' [A principle perpetually reproduced in the Hebrew scriptures already sums up the two conditions of publicity and freedom. The accused man could not be subjected to secret interrogations, where in his confusion, the innocent can furnish deadly weapons against him.][160]

Moreover, Annas had arrogated to himself an illegal position. He had practically made himself the Prisoner's prosecutor; and in Hebrew law it was the duty of the judge to seek for every reason and excuse for releasing—and *not condemning*—the accused, especially if he stood in danger of losing his life.

No witnesses being present, and thus not being able to proceed further with the case, Annas "therefore sent him bound to Caiaphas."[161] By this time it must have been far into the night. The Sanhedrin could not legally sit until after the offering of the sacrifice on the ensuing morning, and because a criminal trial—especially where life was likely to be involved—could not begin, continue, and end on the same day, it would have meant detaining

....

160 *Institutions de Moïse*, i. 366.
161 John 18:24

the Prisoner for at least nine days, owing to the Passover week being followed by a Sabbath. In the meantime, there would be no guarantee that the very multitude who helped to arrest Him, or His own friends from Galilee, might not attempt a rescue and cause a tumult.

Probably these considerations, combined with his fixed determination to put Christ to death, induced Caiaphas to take the illegal course of summoning witnesses and commencing the trial in the palace during the night.

CAIAPHAS THE HIGH PRIEST

Joseph Caiaphas, high priest *de facto* in Jerusalem at the time of our Lord's trial, was the son-in-law and successor of Annas. He was appointed to the Pontifical office by Valerius Gratus in the year A.D. 18, and like most of his predecessors of that period, was removed in due course, in A.D. 36 by Vitellius. There were no less than twenty-eight high priests during a period of one-hundred and sixty years, and Tiberius is reported to have remarked that the rapid way in which new high priests succeeded each other in Jerusalem was exactly "like flies alighting upon a sore." Caiaphas was a Sadducee, and therefore always in conflict with Christ's teaching and bitterly opposed to Him. He was a great friend of Pontius Pilate, and was determined on political issues, if on no others, to sacrifice the Preacher. Hence, we have the anomalous [irregular] and incredible fact, that the very man—who a few hours before had given the order for Christ's arrest for the express purpose of putting Him to death—was now to be the President of the Council of Judges which was to try Him.

Caiaphas was said to be a man of very low intellectual capacity, and his conduct as President of the Sanhedrin during the trial showed him to be one of extremely weak character, and of no moral courage or mental force. He is only once mentioned by name after these events, when, "the rulers and elders and scribes" being gathered together to question Peter and John, Annas is spoken of as the high priest, and Caiaphas is placed among his kindred.[162]

The exact site of the high priest's palace in which the trial took place is not certainly known, though I believe it is considered more than probable that it was situated between the upper city and the Tyropaean Valley. Doubtless Annas and Caiaphas dwelt in the same building, so that when Annas had concluded his interrogation of our Lord, he had simply to send Him to Caiaphas across the uncovered courtyard which is to be found in every Eastern house. The palace would in all probability be in close proximity to the Temple, and the late Sir Charles Wilson has suggested that "it may have been the same place as the house (*oikios*) of Ananias the high priest which was destroyed by the insurgents during the tumult which commenced the war with Rome."[163]

It would consist of suites of apartments built round an open-paved court, and entered from the street through a porch with barred door, at which there would always be a doorkeeper. Probably as in modern Eastern houses, the door would be flanked by a small room on either side, where the servants congregate and chat incessantly. A comparison of the four Gospels points to Annas and Caiaphas living in the same house,[164] and it would be entirely in accordance with Eastern practice where families herd together under one roof, though Annas, as head of the family, probably had his own separate apartments.

Notwithstanding that the Mishna strictly directs that "in capital cases the trial must commence and end in the daytime,"[165] and only trials for money were allowed to be finished at night—Caiaphas, the scribes, elders, and the whole council (*synedrion*)[166] proceeded to commence the trial.

....

162   Acts 4:5-6
163   *Golgotha and the Holy Sepulchre,* p. 39; Josephus, *Wars,* ii. § 6, 17.
164   Matt. 26:57-71; Mark 14:53-68; Luke 22:54-61; John 18:12-25.
165   *De Syn.,* 32; Rabbinowicz, *Législation criminelle du Talmud,* p. 79; Mishna, n. 7.
166   Matt. 25:57,59; Mark 14:53,55.

PROBABLE SEQUENCE OF EVENTS

To fit in the events of that night in their correct sequence is complicated and difficult, the four accounts given by the Evangelists being confused and contradictory.[167] Two of them give first the taking of evidence from false witnesses, which was followed by an attempt to extort a confession. Matthew and Mark read distinctly as if Christ was at once taken to Caiaphas after the arrest, under whose presidency were held two separate trials before the Sanhedrin — one immediately, i.e., during the night, and another on the following morning.[168]

St Luke's account is that they took Him to the palace, where He was mocked and beaten,[169] and that at daybreak[170] the "assembly of the elders," which certainly implies members of the Sanhedrin, led him before "their council" (*synedrion*) who, after asking Him the one crucial question, "Are You the Christ, the Son of God," arose in a body and took Him to Pilate.[171] This evangelist does not mention the false witnesses, though he implies them.

St. John merely states that He was first taken to Annas, who questioned Him and sent Him to Caiaphas, and he omits all mention of a trial before the high priest, saying simply that "they led him from Caiaphas into the Praetorium" in the early morning.[172] Putting together the four narratives the sequence of events seems to be the following:

Christ was first taken to Annas and by him sent on to Caiaphas, where some members of the Sanhedrin having assembled, the false witnesses were brought in. Their evidence failing to "agree together," and therefore no charge being formulated against the Prisoner, the high priest endeavored by putting Him upon

....

167   See Part II of this volume for a chronologically integrated account of the Gospel records of Jesus' trials.
168   Matt. 26:57-27:; Mark 14:55-15:1
169   Luke 22:54,63
170   Luke 23:66
171   Luke 22:70-23:1
172   John 18:24-28

oath[173] to extort a confession which, if He failed to substantiate, practically amounted to "blasphemy against God." Without giving the Prisoner any opportunity of supporting His claim or bringing forward witnesses to prove it, the President at once pronounced Him to be worthy of death,[174] and proceeded to take the votes of the assembled judges, who all condemned Him. These proceedings ended the first trial. In the short time that elapsed between this and the second trial, Christ was tormented by the "officers," (His Jewish guard). At daybreak came the trial before the whole Sanhedrin, but neither Matthew nor Mark state what form that "consultation" took.

Luke's account is that they attempted to obtain practically the same admission from the Prisoner as was extorted at the first trial.[175]

St John omits it altogether.

THE QUESTIONABLE LEGALITY OF THE MORNING SANHEDRIN TRIAL

We must now begin to follow the details of the trial, comparing them with the Jewish law concerning the method of conducting a "trial for life".

To begin with, Salvador in his *Institutions de Moïse* clearly points out that four fundamental principles underlay the whole system of Hebrew criminal jurisprudence as laid down in the Mishna; these were:

    a. Strictness in accusation.

    b. Publicity in discussion.

    c. Full freedom granted to the accused to defend himself.

    d. Assurance against all errors of testimony.

....

173   Matt. 26:63, Mark 14:61
174   Matt. 26:66, mark 14:64
175   Luke 22:67-70

These points we must keep clearly before us throughout the whole proceedings.

It has been first of all contended by some writers that the trial being held in the high priest's palace invalidated it, but given that forty years before the court had given up sitting in the Lishcath ha Gazith, the Talmud recognizes the legality of the high priest's palace as a place of session. Strictly speaking, not less than twenty-three members should have been present *the whole time* to take part in a trial for life; but it is unlikely that being in the dead of night this regulation was adhered to. Also, the fact that on the next morning the Prisoner was taken before the 'whole council' seems to imply that the necessary quorum was not present at the night sitting.

It is possible that messengers had been dispatched during the night apprising the seventy-one members of the great Sanhedrin of the arrest of Christ, and that they consequently mustered in strong force in the morning. It must be admitted that it was a grave breach of the law that the trial was begun at night. "Judgments in souls are conducted by day, and must be settled by day,'" moreover the great Sanhedrin might only sit during the hours of daylight.

The judgment being set, let us turn first to the Mishna and learn from its pages what ought to have been the proper course for the Council to pursue, comparing it with what actually transpired as stated in the gospels.

THE IMPORTANCE OF THE WITNESSES

First the witnesses who *must be voluntary* are instructed to bring in their prisoner and state their evidence against him. As there could be no sole judge, so must there be no "sole witness,"[176] and before all things the accusation must be publicly made. A Hebrew trial was practically a public duet between the judges and the witnesses. To use modern legal phraseology, there were no such persons as Counsel for the prosecution, and Counsel

---

176   Deut. 19:15-18

for the defendant. The witnesses—two at least—must bring the arrested man into court on their own initiative, and there state his crime. Until they *publicly* formulated their evidence against him before the tribunal, he was to all intents and purposes innocent—I might almost say unaccused. The evidence of the witnesses was practically the accusation; there was no such thing as a formal indictment before the judges.

The witnesses having stated on oath their charge, those for the defense were at once called upon to speak, and the defendant himself might say anything he liked on his own behalf. It was also permitted for any of the scholars present if they could say anything in favor of the accused to do so, but they could not say anything— even if they could prove it— to his disadvantage. If what they stated seemed likely to be to the point, the judges are directed to call them to take a place beside them on the bench, where they must remain during the trial. Subsequently they were to be put on oath—which they were allowed to take sitting—and their statements were then carefully sifted. No cross-examination was permitted as the trial was a conflict of evidences, but the onus of proving the accused as guilty lay upon the shoulders of *those who arrested him*. So completely were they made to feel the grave responsibility of their act that, before giving their evidence, they were bound over to tell the truth by a most solemn oath, and, in the event of capital punishment ensuing, the two principal witnesses had to cast the first stones at the condemned man. The judges were essentially in the position of counsel for the accused. Their duty was to *protect him* by every means in their power, and with all the precautions, quibbles, and sanctions contained in the Mishna it is a wonder is that anyone ever suffered the death penalty.

To all intents and purposes, it was the Sanhedrin who prosecuted Christ *by seeking for false witnesses* in order that they might put him to death—two flagrant breaches of the law, the former being, as Taylor Innes observes in his admirable *Legal Monograph*, "a scandalous indecorum." A stranger sight can seldom have been seen in the High Court of Jewry than that of the judges sending out to seek for witnesses, in order to be able to proceed against a prisoner whom they had ordered to be arraigned before them for a pre-determined verdict.

METHOD OF CRIMINAL PROCEDURE

The tractate, *De Synhedris*, gives us precise details as to the method to be pursued in criminal cases. Although the Talmud was not reduced to writing until many years after this famous trial took place, and although it is possible that under the Roman Government of Judea some restrictions in, or variations of, procedure may have been made, the consensus of learned Jewish opinion is that in all important points the regulations were laid down, and obtained in the reign of Tiberius.

Jewish trials were, roughly speaking, divided into two classes:

Money Trials and Trials for Life, or, as they are also called, Trials in Souls. Money Trials and Trials for Life had the same rules of enquiry and investigation. But they differed in procedure on the following points:

1. Money Trials require only three judges, while Trials for Life required twenty-three judges.

2. In Money Trials, it matters not on which side the judges speak, who give the first opinions; in Trials for Life, those who are in favor of acquittal must speak first.

3. In Money Trials, a majority of one is always enough; in Trials for Life a majority of one is enough to acquit, but it requires a majority of two to condemn.

4. In Money Trials, a decision may be quashed on review (for error) no matter which way it has gone; in Trials for Life a condemnation may be quashed, but not an acquittal.

5. In Money Trials, disciples of the law present in the court may speak — as assessors — on either side; in Trials for Life, they may speak in favor of the accused, but not against him.

6. In Money Trials, a judge who has indicated his opinion, no matter on which side, may change his mind; in Trials for Life, he who has given his voice for guilt may change his

mind, but not he who has given his voice for acquittal.

7. Money Trials are commenced only in the daytime, but may be concluded after nightfall; Trials for Life are commenced only in the daytime, and must also be concluded during the daytime.

8. Money Trials may be concluded by either acquittal or condemnation on the day on which they have begun; Trials for Life may be concluded on that day, if there is a sentence of acquittal, but must be postponed to a second day if there is to be a condemnation to death. *For this reason, capital trials are not held on the day before a Sabbath or a feast day.*

9. In Money Trials, they begin by asking the opinion of the eldest; in Trials for Life, with those who sit at the side.

10. "All are qualified to judge trials for money, but not everyone is qualified to judge a trial for life — only priests, Levites, and those Israelites who may legally marry priests' daughters are thus qualified."[177]

If the evidence offered on behalf of the accused is sufficiently cogent [convincing], the judges proceed to vote at once, and acquit and dismiss him. If not, the trial must be postponed until the following day, when the witnesses against the prisoner are put on oath, and their evidence is subjected to a most searching investigation.

"If a man is found innocent, the court absolves him. But if not, his judgment is put off until the following day. Meantime the judges go out, and meeting outside the court they confer together all night, eating but little food and drinking no wine. On the following morning they return into court and vote over again with the like precautions as before."[178]

The Mishna defines carefully those persons whose relationships or affinities to the accused shall preclude them from giving evidence against him, and also those whose proclivities shall disqualify them: Brothers, uncles, brothers-in-law, father-in-law, stepfather,

177   *De Syn.*, iv. 1.
178   *De Syn.*, v. 1.

and uncles by marriage, merchants who trade in the Sabbatic year, moneylenders, gamblers, and those who bet on the flight of doves.[179]

The judges having satisfied themselves that not any of these disqualifications exist, next proceed to adjure [swear in] each witness separately in the following solemn words:

"Forget not, O witness, that it is one thing to give evidence in a trial for money, and another in a trial for life. In a money suit, if thy witness bearing shall do wrong, money may repair that wrong. But in this trial for life, if you sin, the blood of the accused and the blood of his seed unto the end of time shall be imputed onto you. . . . Therefore was Adam created, one man and alone, to teach thee that if any shall destroy one soul out of Israel, he is held by the scripture to be as if he had destroyed the world. . . . For a man from one signet ring, may strike off many impressions, and all of them shall be exactly alike. But He, the King of Kings, He the Holy and Blessed, has struck off from His type of the first man the forms of all men that shall live; yet so, that no one human being is wholly alike to any other. Wherefore let us think and believe that the whole world was created for such a man as he whose life hangs on thy words."

If after this, the witness feels he dare not take the oath, he is to be dismissed immediately and sent outside the court; but should he say, "I will nevertheless swear," he shall stand up, and in a language which he understands, take the oath by "the Lord the God of heaven."

Before, however, he actually takes it, the court is directed once again to warn the witness in the following words:

"Be aware that the oath which you take is not according to your own mind, but to the mind of the Omnipotent and of the court; as Moses said: 'And not with you only do I make this covenant and this oath, but with Him that stands here with us this day.'"[180]

....

179   *De Syn.*, iii. 3,4.

180   Deut. 29:14-15

A small body of the judges shall then privately examine each witness in turn; and having satisfied themselves that the evidence is relevant and suitable, shall bring him into court, where each one separately and without being heard by others, is to make his statements in the presence of the accused.

FORMS OF ORAL EVIDENCE

Jewish law recognized three forms of oral evidence:

A. A vain testimony.

B. A standing testimony.

C. An equal or adequate testimony [the witnesses' statements must agree with each other].

The first was practically worthless and not even provisionally [temporarily] taken into account by the judges. The second was considered as sufficiently relevant to be allowed to stand provisionally, in case subsequent [later] facts confirmed it, when it was permitted to complete the evidence as adequate testimony. The third was the words of them that agree together, and the smallest discrepancy was held to invalidate it.[181]

If the witness perjured himself [lied], the punishment was, "Ye shall do unto him as he had thought to do unto his brother."[182]

VOTING PROCEDURE

The evidence having been taken and the witnesses for the defense having been heard, the judges then proceeded to vote, beginning with the youngest members seated at the ends of the semicircle, the casting vote being given by the President.

"If the judges find a good reason to acquit him (the accused), they do so immediately; and if not, they postpone the trial until the morrow. If twelve of them acquit and eleven condemn, he is

---

181 *De Syn.* V. 3,4.
182 Deut. 19: 18-19; Susanna, 61-62

acquitted. But if twelve condemn and eleven acquit, and even if eleven condemn and eleven acquit, but the twenty-third says, 'I am in doubt' even if twenty-two are for condemning or acquitting, and one says, 'I do not know,' judges are to be added. And to what number? Two and two till the whole number reaches seventy-one, and then if thirty-six acquit and thirty-five condemn, he is acquitted; but if thirty-six condemn and thirty-five acquit, the discussion is prolonged in case one of those who condemns later changes his mind. If and when judgment is at last pronounced, they bring out the man sentenced, and stone him. The place of punishment is to be apart from the place of judgment, for it is said in Leviticus 24:14, 'Bring the blasphemer [outside] the camp.'"[183]

THE PUNISHMENT

The original method of stoning was for the principal witness to cast the first stone at the condemned man; if this did not prove fatal, the bystanders then hurled stones at him until death ensued. In our Lord's time it was different; the criminal was thrown down from a height; the Bêt-ha-Sêkala or stoning place being twice the height of a man. The chief witness grasping him firmly by the thighs thrust him backwards in such a manner that he fell on his back. Should he, however, fall face downwards, he must be turned over. It was only in the event of the fall not proving fatal that all Israel, i.e., the bystanders, "stoned him with stones till he died." The body was buried under a cairn[184] outside the city gates or in a common burial place belonging to the Sanhedrin, and the relatives were allowed later on to gather together the bones for interment in the family tomb. If the criminal was put to death for being either a blasphemer or an idolater, the corpse was at once gibbeted[185] until sunset, and then buried.[186]

So greatly was capital punishment deprecated [disapproved of] by the Talmud that, after the procession had started for the place

....

183 *De Syn.*, v. vi.
184 Man-made piles of stones used as a burial mound or grave marker.
185 Put on display, whether on a stake, gallows, or cross.
186 *De Syn.*, xii. 3; Josephus, *Antiq.*, iv. 8; Jewish Encyclopaedia on 'Capital Punishment'.

of execution, it was possible to save the condemned man; and arrangements were made for a reprieve being granted *even when* near the stoning place.

"An officer shall stand at the door of the court with a flag in his hand; another mounted shall follow the procession so far, but shall halt at the furthest point where he can see the man with the flag (the judges remain sitting), and if any one offers to prove that the condemned man is innocent, he at the door shall wave the flag, and the horseman instantly shall gallop after the condemned and recall him for his defense. Even if the condemned man himself says, 'I have something more to say in my defense,' he is to be brought back to the court even four or five times provided there is something in it which is worthy of consideration."[187]

From the above quotations from the Mishna, it will be seen what careful precautions — I might almost say exaggerated precautions — were taken in order to preserve the life of every Hebrew citizen, and to ensure him strict justice.

THE QUESTION OF ADHERENCE TO THE LAW

Was the law adhered to in the trial of Jesus Christ?

Let us turn to the Gospels and compare the actual proceedings of the court, with those that we have seen *should* have taken place.

Instead of the witnesses bringing in their prisoner, "they that had taken him," i.e., the emissaries of His judges brought Him before the Council, and those who should have been His protectors "*sought* false witnesses to put him to death," and found them not, for though many came forward and bare witness against Him, their testimony was not "adequate."[188] Two men at last were found whose words were evidently regarded as "standing testimony", though in the end it proved to be an inadequate or "not equal" testimony.

....

187   *De Syn.*, v. 5; vi. 1
188   Matt. 26:59, Mark 14:55

These witnesses were then sworn, and their evidence elicited by the series of questions known as *Hakiroth*:

    a. In what Sabbatic period did you hear so-and-so say this thing?
    b. In what year of the Sabbatic period?
    c. In what month?
    d. On what date of the month?
    e. On what day of the week?
    f. At what hour?
    g. In what place?

These would be followed by another set called *Bedikoth*, which were of purely secondary importance, but useful for purposes of comparison in weighing a standing testimony.

The witnesses swore that they heard him say:

    a. "I am able to destroy the Temple of God and build (*oikodomeō*) it in three days." Matt. 26:61

    b. "I will destroy this Temple that is made with hands, and in three days I will build (*oikodomeō*) another made without hands." Mark 14:58

What Christ really did say is recorded in the fourth Gospel, in John 2:19-21:
"Destroy this Temple and in three days I will raise (*egeirō*) it up," but he spoke of the Temple of his body. Christ [was putting] the case hypothetically: "If *you* destroy *I* will raise up."

These witnesses twisted the sense round to "I *will* destroy and in three days rebuild without hands."

By Hebrew law "the least discordance between the evidence of witnesses was held to destroy its value."[189]

---

189   Even the smallest inconsistency rendered the testimony invalid. Salvador, *Inst. De Moïse*, i. 373.

The first charge, if substantiated, was *sorcery*, for only by Satanic agency could the massive building, which it had taken forty and six years to rear, be rebuilt in three days. The punishment for sorcery was death.

The second charge included more than sorcery. The destruction of their beloved Temple, their pride and joy, and the dwelling place of Jehovah, would be sacrilege as well, and, to a theocratic commonwealth like the Jewish-- *blasphemy*. The punishment for that was stoning and exposure of the body.

The evidence being inconclusive it was now the duty of the President to dismiss the Prisoner or bid Him bring forward witnesses on His side; and at the same time sentence the false witnesses to death. Instead of doing this, the high priest proceeded to commit a grave breach of that very law his exalted position alone should have prevented him from doing. Nor can ignorance be pleaded as an excuse in his case, for as *ex-officio* President of the Sanhedrin he must, by years of study and practice of the law, have been intimately acquainted with its every detail and intricacy. Caiaphas—the chief judge—now began himself to question the Prisoner before him—a proceeding which was absolutely illegal. "Are you not going to answer? What is this testimony that these men are bringing against you?"

And this from him whose bounden duty it was not only to do all in his power to protect the life of the accused, and even to refuse to accept a confession of guilt unless it was proved by the adequate testimony of two, if not three, witnesses!

In such a hopelessly unjust trial, Jesus Christ quietly refused to take any part, and His dignified silence is far more impressive than the most eloquent defense. It was, at the same time, a tacit reminder to His judges that they were impugning the rights of a Hebrew citizen, to whom the Bench should address no question. Christ's silence was the keeping of the law.

At this crisis the Sanhedrin appear to have got thoroughly out of hand. The failure of the witnesses to produce an adequate testimony had evidently exasperated them. Hostile and illegal questions were hurled at the Prisoner, with the intent to make him incriminate Himself, while the very ground of the inquiry was shifted. They now began to ask Him if He was the Christ, the Son of God, and the Son of the Blessed. It was the old question once more brought forward, and again later on repeated before the Great Sanhedrin.[190]

Then was enacted a scene which — were it not so terribly tragic — might almost be called theatrical. It looks as if at this crisis, Caiaphas, infuriated at his unsuccessful attempts to prove the Prisoner guilty of death, completely lost his head. Thwarted at every turn, he seems to have become overpowered with rage. He had already violated every point of criminal procedure in order to gain his end, and yet the Prisoner before him was, in the eyes of their law, an unaccused man and ought to have been released.

Instead of setting Him at liberty Caiaphas stood up and administered to the Prisoner the most solemn form of oath it was possible to make — an oath so solemn that it was administered sometimes, when all else failed, to criminals of a desperate type, in order to extort finally a true confession of their crimes.

It was a wholly unjustifiable step, but Christ accepting as a pious Jew the awful responsibility thrust upon Him, answered simply, "I am; and you someday shall see the Son of Man sitting at the right hand of power, and coming in the clouds of heaven."

This was the supreme moment for the Jewish nation. On oath, the weightiest any Hebrew could make, Christ avowed himself before the highest tribunal in His country, and under the very shadow of Jehovah's dwelling-place, to be the Son of the Blessed, their Messiah and their King. Either the Prisoner at the bar was in truth that which He claimed to be — the long-looked-for hope of Israel, or else He blasphemed Jehovah.

....
190   Luke 22:67

No one, however, paused to ask for His credentials, no man asked Him then as they had in former days, "What sign can you show us that we may believe?" None inquired of themselves "What and if, after all, this should be the Deliverer?" Without even suggesting that He should prove His words, Caiaphas exclaimed: "He has spoken blasphemy. Behold now you have heard His blasphemy." When a man blasphemed the God of Israel, the judges were directed to arise and rend their outer garment from the neck downwards, with a rent that never again was to be sewn together.[191] This Caiaphas did, and turning as directed by the law to either side of the semicircle, he put the momentous question first to right and then to left.

For life?

For death?

And all replied:

Ish Maveth, i.e., a man of death.[192]

"So passed that great condemnation." A condemnation that was to change the whole aspect of future history—and to influence untold generations that were yet to come—a condemnation which meant the rejection by the Sanhedrin of their Messiah in the name of and before the whole Jewish nation, and after a trial that was illegal in every detail.

THE SECOND CONDEMNATION

At this point the meeting was adjourned until the early morning, when Christ was led before the whole council—not to be retried—but merely to give an appearance of legality to the former proceedings, for the decision to condemn *must not be arrived at during the night*.

....

191   *De Syn.*, vii. 6, 11
192   I am aware that Joseph of Arimathea "had not consented to their counsel and deed," but it is not certain that he formed one of the tribunal that night.

As a matter of fact, the Great Sanhedrin could not meet until after the offering of the morning sacrifice, neither — presuming that the crucifixion took place on the Friday — could they sit legally on that day, being that on which the Passover Lamb was eaten; nor had they the right to pass the final sentence of death upon a cause which had been tried that very day.[193]

To all intents and purposes, the judges contented themselves with the mere repetition of the question asked a few hours earlier,

"If you are the Christ, tell us", to which he calmly answered, "If I do tell you, you will not believe me."

"Are you then the Son of God?" they once more demanded, to which question, "You say that I am," was His quiet reply.

On the face of it the answer looks evasive, but in reality it is far from it. It was once more an illegal demand by the judges for a confession, which the law emphatically forbade; and the "You say so," was the gentle reminder that the duty of the judges was to ask the witnesses (His accusers) to come forward and make their charge, and not the Prisoner. Again the council declared that He blasphemed God, and they ratified the judgment passed at the former session.

Thus, for the second time, the Jewish nation, by the voice of its rulers, rejected the Messiah.

Jesus Christ was condemned to death for blasphemy; because on a confession illegally extorted from Him: He admitted that He was the Son of God.

According to Maimonides it was contrary to Jewish law to sentence a prisoner to death on his own confession.

Salvador says upon this point: "*Notre loi ne condamne jamais sur le simple aveu de l'accusé.*" (Our law never convicts on the simple admission of the accused.)

The Rabbi Bartenora in a note to *De Syn.*, vi. 2 writes: "It

---

193   The Jewish day was reckoned from sunset to sunset.

is a fundamental principle with us that no one can damage himself by what he says during judgment."

Cocceius also states "*Ita tenent Magistri, neminem ex propria confessione aut prophetae vaticinio esse neci dandum.*" (Thus the masters hold that no one should be put to death on account of his own confession or the prophecy of the prophet.)

THE DEFINITION OF BLASPHEMY

Now comes the question, what constituted blasphemy?

In its earlier sense, it was an offense or insult against God. In its later and more developed meaning, it became any form of offense which actively or constructively set itself in opposition to or "struck at" Jehovah — the invisible though potential King of the Jewish theocracy. At the same time the sacred Name, the tetragrammaton JHVH, *must be mentioned.*

> "*Nemo tenctur blasphemus nisi expressit nomen.*"[194] (No one is held to be a blasphemer unless he has expressed the Name).

> Practically it was "*Crimen laesae majestatis divinae*", i.e., treason against the Deity.

Looking at the purely legal aspect of the case, and putting aside all theological meanings which have been attached to the expression "Son of God", it is quite clear that there was no high treason against Jehovah in claiming to be the Messiah, nor even in asserting Sonship with God Himself, *provided that it could be proved.* While, on the other hand, the outrageous audacity of making such a stupendous claim, and not being able to substantiate it, would constitute treason against the Deity in the highest degree.

The Sanhedrin were in duty bound to consider the Messianic identity of the Accused. There was every reason why the claim should be fully and openly weighed, for Scripture, prophecy, tradition, and the whole feeling of the nation pointed to the speedy appearance of the Messiah.

....
194   *De Syn.*, vii. 6, 11

But the problem was not even for one moment considered; the Messiah was summarily rejected as a blasphemer, and sentenced to death.

His judges sought pretexts for condemning Him and not proofs of His guilt, and they undoubtedly hurried the trial for fear of a popular demonstration in His favor.

THE POWER OF THE SANHEDRIN

It has been very ably contended that the Sanhedrin had no legal power to try and pass sentence of death upon Jesus Christ; and it is a contention which must receive attention. Rosadi says: "The sole authority that could try Jesus, arrest and examine Him and render Him amenable to the consequences of his alleged offense," was the Roman Procurator; and he quotes Carmignani and Lémann to back up his opinion. Dupin also holds that the "Jewish court had no right to try for grave or at least capital crimes at all"; that their procedure was a usurpation (taking power that was not theirs).

On the other hand, Mommsen declares that they had every right to do so, and Salvador the learned Spanish Rabbi, says: "The Jews retained the faculty of trying cases according to their own law, but it was only the Roman Procurator that had executive power. No culprit could be executed without his consent." Maimonides and Rabbinowicz are also of this opinion.

Around this much vexed question there has grown up a perfect mountain of literature, and there is no doubt that even now opinions vary considerably, but there are a few points, more perhaps of common-sense than of law, that may be taken into account, in trying to arrive at a decision.

I. Christ was tried for an ecclesiastical [religious/church] offence; and it seems to be fairly established that the Romans, in matters affecting religious questions, allowed the Jews the right of trial in first instance, retaining for themselves the right of *recognitio* did they wish to exercise it. It was an understood thing, of course, that the Roman Procurator alone could actually deliver over a prisoner to death. The *jus gladii*[195] passed away from the Jewish people with the advent [arrival] of Roman power.

II. Annas the ex-high priest, had been deposed only a few years before by Pilate's predecessor for putting certain prisoners to death during his absence. It is hardly likely that the Sanhedrin by stretching their privileges again would have so soon risked losing them.

While there was no *concordat* [agreement] between the Jews and the Romans, the latter undoubtedly allowed the conquered nation to exercise their own religion and carry out their ecclesiastical and ceremonial law within their own borders, and so long as there was no infringement of the prerogatives of Imperial Caesar, a fair amount both of freedom and power were left to the Sanhedrin. It was ever the policy of Rome in dealing with her colonies and foreign dependencies to allow great latitude [freedom] to their ruling officials in the matter of religious questions.

From a Roman point of view the Jews had no *rights*, but they certainly were allowed privileges.

III. If the Sanhedrin had exceeded their privileges, Pilate would certainly have tried the whole case *de novo* [anew] with a formal Roman trial; and at the same time would undoubtedly have manifested his displeasure.

IV. It is generally conceded by the greater number of writers, that during the troublous period of the Hasmonaeans, certain modifications crept into the legal practices of the Jews, some of which were done away with under Roman rule. Therefore, in judging the conduct of the Sanhedrin, we must make a little allowance for the regulations of the Mishna not being strictly adhered to. Herod I., King of Judea in B.C. 40, the first Roman successor of the Hasmonaeans, was very jealous of the Sanhedrin, and tried to curtail [end] their privileges. After the deposition

---

195   Supreme jurisdiction. The right to absolve from, or condemn a man to death.

of Archelaus in A.D. 6 and the appointment of Procurators, much of their ecclesiastical and municipal power was restored to them; but in matters imperial and political, the Jews were eminently the conquered people, from whom Rome brooked neither suggestion nor interference.

Jerusalem was practically governed by the priestly party, and therefore by the Sadducees who were a political set, it being clearly understood that they in no way infringed their privileges, duly paid the imperial taxes, avoided any contravention of Roman laws, and kept good order within the city. Close to the Temple stood the fortress of Antonia in which six thousand soldiers are said to have been always quartered[196] with the main force of the legionaries at Caesarea Stratonis nearby, so that any breach of the peace or case of maladministration, at once met with summary punishment. The Jews were notorious for their lawlessness and for being ever on the verge of revolt; in fact, so little did the Romans trust them that at the Feasts, a strong body of troops was always brought into Jerusalem.

Taking all these points into consideration it is not likely that the Sanhedrin or Caiaphas would have desired to break their friendship with Pilate. The Jewish rulers had been left the privilege of trying and condemning a prisoner for an ecclesiastical offence, and they used it, but they could go no further. They might verbally consign Christ to the most cruel death you can possibly imagine, but they had not the power to hurt one single hair of His head. Caesar alone by the mouth of his Procurator could issue the death warrant, and therefore to Pilate must the Sanhedrin go for permission to put Jesus Christ to death.

PONTIUS PILATE

"Colui che fece per viltate il gran rifiuto A Deo spiacento ed ai nemici sui." (I worshiped him through cowardice, the great rejection of God and his enemies.)

---

196   Josephus, *Wars*, v. 5, 8.

At the time of the birth of Jesus Christ, Syria was divided into three parts for governmental purposes. Idumaea, Samaria, and Judea were administered by Archelaus until A.D. 6, when Augustus deposed and banished him to Gaul — Publius Sulpicius Quirinius succeeding him.[197] In Galilee and Peraea, Herod Antipas was tetrarch until Caligula relegated him in A.D. 39 to Lugdunum; and Philip governed the barren regions of the extreme northern border. From the time of Quirinius, Judea was placed under the administration of Rome itself, as a province of Syria, and a *Procurator Caesaris cum potestate*[198], armed with plenary powers, governed the province in the name of, and was directly responsible to the Imperator himself.[199] In Jerusalem the high priest, in conjunction with the Sanhedrin, presided over purely Jewish affairs and matters ecclesiastical.

Lucius Pontius Pilate, the Procurator Caesaris in Judea at the time of Christ's trial, is one of those characters concerning whom but little historical is known, yet of whom any number of traditional stories are told. It is said, but on doubtful authority, that he was a Spaniard, born in Seville. He was a soldier and the son of a distinguished soldier, and after fighting in Germany under Germanicus, went to Rome on amusement bent. While there he fell in love with and married Claudia Procula, the illegitimate daughter of Claudia the third wife of Tiberius, and the granddaughter of Augustus Caesar. When appointed Governor of Judea, Pontius Pilate asked for, and obtained, the unusual permission to take his wife with him. Of his rule in Judea, we know hardly anything authentic. We learn from Josephus that he annoyed the Jews by causing the *insignia* of Caesar to be set up in the sacred city, and that again later he incurred their hatred by appropriating some of the Temple funds for the useful and highly necessary work of bringing water into the city, a work which met with no sympathy from them. The water supply of Jerusalem was at the best of times but scanty, and with the greatly increased population caused by the Roman occupation, wholly inadequate. He is said to have also dealt severely with the Samaritans, who having been beguiled by a foolish impostor

....

197   Luke 2:2
198   Caesar's Manager with power.
199   Tacitus, *Annals*, ii. 66; Suetonius, *Tiberius*, 22.

promising to produce the sacred vessels hidden in Mount Gerizim, armed themselves to assemble there in force. Pilate knowing the turbulent nature of the people, and being responsible for the maintenance of peace and quiet, stole a march upon them in order to prevent a riot; and on the arrival of the Samaritans at the Mount, they found it surrounded by Roman soldiers, who dispersed the mob, capturing many, and putting the ringleaders to death.[200]

Owing to representations made to Vitellius, the Governor of Syria, Pilate was ordered to Rome to give an account of himself to Caesar, but on his arrival Tiberius was dead. Cassiodorus says that he was banished to Vena Gallica, where he died. Two letters and a report are extant purporting to be from Pontius Pilate to Tiberius, relating to the trial of Jesus Christ, but they are in Greek, not Latin, and though they are interesting up to a certain point, can only be regarded as apocryphal. Beyond these few facts, and the conduct of the Procurator himself towards Christ as shown in the Gospels, we have no clue to the personality of the man. He has been made the object of unrivaled condemnation throughout the ages, from ecclesiastics and historians alike; and Josephus and Philo his biographers, are so violent in their language concerning him that we are driven to the conclusion that many of their statements cannot be accepted as historical.

Pilate was placed in a position of very great difficulty, and one requiring much firmness and decision, and he failed, and it is not easy at this distance of time to weigh impartially and accurately the guilt of the heathen governor. I hold no brief [support] for Pontius Pilate, and I have not the slightest intention of whitewashing his character, but at least let us be fair to the man; and while we sternly condemn the injustice of Caiaphas and the Sanhedrin, let us not fail in seeing that justice is meted out even to Pilate the failure.

In judging of his conduct towards Christ, we have to remember how different a view of the matter the Pagan governor would have taken from either the Sanhedrin, or a Christian council. Pilate's first and foremost duty was to preserve order in a conquered

....
200   Josephus, *Antiq*. xviii.; 4, 1.

country whose inhabitants were proverbial [known] for their disaffection and insubordination, and were moreover a people whom he cordially disliked. The religions of the two races were also fundamentally antagonistic, though never likely to clash, for Rome, while worshipping at her own altars in Judea, left the Jews in peace to serve Jehovah in their own land, and the latter for their part never desired to proselytize.[201] Consequently, Pilate knew nothing of the Jewish faith and probably cared less.

He was a low-born Roman soldier of no mental culture[202], who would be completely ignorant as to what blasphemy against God meant, or what a vital question was involved in the assumption by the Prisoner of the title "Son of God." His duty as Procurator was to take into consideration two points: Was the Prisoner guilty of treason against Caesar, and was He, by His religious doctrines and teaching, stirring up revolt and sedition among His fellow-countrymen? The first of these Pilate dismissed with a verdict of not guilty; and the second was not even worth a thought.

There was no injustice nor even unfairness in sending Christ to Herod — the superior officer — though legally there was no necessity for it. Pilate was merely trying to shirk responsibility under the cloak of deference.

Pilate's failure as a judge was that he had not strength of mind to carry out his just verdict of "I find no crime in him."

So in the grey dawn of that early April morning, the chief priests, with the elders and scribes, accompanied by a crowd of Jews,[203] passed with their Prisoner across the Temple precincts. Opinions differ as to which palace Pilate was at this time inhabiting. It was not likely to have been — as many suggest — the Castle of Antonia, as that contained the barracks and so was not at all suitable as the residence of a Roman lady of Imperial birth. It may have been

---

201   The Jews typically do not evangelize or try and convince others to convert to Judaism.
202   Possessing an understanding of other cultures, being "worldly" in today's vernacular.
203   Luke 23:4

the beautiful palace built by Herod the Great, which with its fine marble court would make an excellent place for Roman open-air trials. This lay near the present gardens of the Armenian patriarch, and was connected with the Temple by a causeway across the Tyropaean Valley. As Herod, the tetrarch of Galilee, had come to Jerusalem for the Feast, it is not impossible that Pilate, wishing to do him honor, may have ceded the palace to him for temporary use, and have gone himself with his wife into the old palace of the Hasmonaeans, built on a fine spur on the west side of the Temple, and therefore quite easy of access.

At any rate one thing is certain, and that is that the Praetorium was wherever Pilate at that moment resided, the name being applied in the first instance to the Praetor's tent of older and simpler days, then to the military council, and finally, after the days of Augustus, to the building where the Procurator was at that time. Into the palace court that Christ's judges, who had not hesitated to break the law on most vital points, had scruples against entering. Had they done so they would have been defiled, and unable to eat the Passover.[204] So standing before the balustrade, which separated the palace from the Temple precincts, they awaited the moment when the *bema* or portable chair, in which the Roman magistrates sat when administering justice, should be put in place, and the Procurator appear.

Pilate as a concession to Jewish religious feelings went out to them, and at once with the true Roman spirit of fair play demanded: "What accusation do you bring?" The Sanhedrin evaded the question by replying that He was an "evil-doer," literally a malefactor, upon which Pilate, evidently thinking that it was merely some local or religious offence, bade the Jews judge Him according to their own law. He probably thought as did—later on—Annaeus Gallio, the pro-consul of Achaia, that "if it were a matter of wrong or wicked villainy of you Jews, reason would that I should bear with you, but if it be a question of words and names and of your own law, you see to it, I will be no judge in these matters."[205]

....

204   This points to the crucifixion not having taken place on the Friday.
205   Acts 13:14-15

This brought the accusers to their bearings, and they were obliged to return the galling answer: "It is not permissible for us to put any one to death." It was the bitter admission unwillingly wrung from them, that they were a conquered people, and could not execute their own law. It at once gave Pilate a clue to the whole situation, though his question: "What accusation?" still remained unanswered. My belief is that Caiaphas, being a friend of Pilate, hoped that the Procurator would have accepted the judgment of the Sanhedrin without further enquiry, and signed the necessary permission, or perhaps he trusted that out of consideration for their religious scruples at the Passover time, and knowing how prone the people were to riot during the feasts, Pilate would, for the sake of quiet and order, have at once condemned the Prisoner to death. The high priest may also have feared a reversal of the sentence. It is evident from the first that the Roman governor meant to use his right of *recognitio*, all the more so that he could not obtain a direct answer to his question. They "accused him of many things," but nothing definite.

At last, the Procurator succeeded in getting a statement of the Prisoner's crime, but the ground of the accusation had once more shifted. This time it was not sorcery and blasphemy with which Christ was charged, but with treason against great Caesar himself—a crime which the rulers knew would immediately compel the attention of the Procurator.

a. "We found him perverting the nation."
b. "Forbidding to give tribute to Caesar."
c. "Saying He is Christ a king."

Having first accused him in a vague way of evil *doing*, they now definitely state evil *speaking* in three ways.

The first count Pilate cared nothing about; it did not matter one iota to imperial Rome that a religious fanatic should pervert the Jewish nation. The second was too obviously false to stand; it had already been brought up and disproved.[206]

....

206   Mark 12:17

The third, if true, was very serious; it was nothing short of *Crimen laesae Majestatis* — a crime which Tiberius punished with the utmost severity, and concerning which had even issued an edict that verbal statements as well as overt acts were to be counted as treason, while to use the sacred name of Caesar was to give a yet more serious aspect to the case.[207]

If Christ had been a Roman citizen, the mere verbal accusation would not have availed against him as a case of treason must be attested by the production of the written libel; but not being able to claim, as did St. Paul, the privilege: *"Civis Romanus sum"* (I am a Roman citizen), He, as one of a conquered nation was defenseless, and could only trust the justice of His judge.

Having extracted a definite statement of crime from the Prisoner's accusers, Pilate proceeded at once to put the right and natural question: "Are you the king of the Jews?" to which Christ replied, "You say that I am." Comparing the four Gospels, it seems as if this interrogation and reply must have taken place in the hearing of the chief priests, elders, and the multitude who were accusing him, some of one thing and some of another. Pilate in despair at getting at the truth of the matter with all the confusion going on round him, appealed to the Prisoner himself and finally with drew him into the Praetorium, where he could quietly investigate the charge.

The judge again put the same question: "Are you the king of the Jews?" Christ's answer when alone with the Procurator is most interesting. He first asks His judge a question "Do you say this of your own accord, or did others say it to you about me?" In other words, Christ asks his judge: "Do you as the representative of Caesar ask me, if I stand here at your judgment seat guilty of attacking the Roman power and claiming to be the King of the Jews in the place of the Imperator; or is it merely because others tell you I am the king of the Jews that you ask me?"

It was but a few days before that Christ had sternly bidden the spies

....

207   Tacitus, *Annals*, i. 39

sent by the high priests and elders to "take hold of his speech" to "render to Caesar the things which are Caesar's," making it quite clear that the kingdom over which He proclaimed Himself a King was not to be established by means of the overthrow of the powers that be. He had, in fact, pointed out that although in days to come, Christianity might find itself in collision with empires and powers in high places, it was no part of His plan of campaign to destroy the kingdoms of the world in order to establish His own. His kingdom was not to be founded upon the ruins of lawfully constituted authority.

Pilate, a Roman, naturally retorted: "Am I a Jew? Your own nation and the chief priests have delivered you over to me. What have you done?" Practically, if Christ of Himself claimed to be the King of the Jews, then there might be political mischief lurking behind, and treason against Caesar might have been committed; but if others said He was the King of the Jews, then probably it was nothing but yet another of those fanatical religious movements which were always stirring in Judea, and Pilate could dismiss the Prisoner as innocent.

Christ's reply was at once Eastern and symbolical: "My kingdom is not of this *kosmos,* otherwise my servants would fight that I should not be delivered into the hands of the Jews." Pilate still puzzled, reiterated the question: "Are you then a king?" and Christ admitted that He was a King, and was born into the world to bear witness to the truth. Pilate more puzzled still, and still less understanding the Prisoner's meaning, but quite convinced that here was no political crime to be punished, exclaimed hopelessly: "What is the truth of the matter?" and going out to the angry crowd said: "I find no crime in Him." It was quite evident to the prosaic and unlettered mind of the Roman governor that this self-styled King was but the imaginary ruler of a phantom kingdom — a product of His brain alone. He might be a fanatic or a madman, or even both, but He was certainly no evil-doer, nor was He plotting against Caesar.

The charge had broken down — Pilate was bound to acquit the

prisoner, and he did so.[208] Thus far the Procurator had been an absolutely just judge.

THE VERDICT

The verdict "I find no crime in Him" appears to have raised a perfect storm, and priests and people alike clamored for the death sentence. Matthew and John state that Pilate now proposed the alternative release of Jesus or Barabbas the murderer. Mark says that the multitude "began to ask him (Pilate) to do as he was wont to do unto them," and that the chief priests stirred up the people "that he should rather release Barabbas unto them" begging that Jesus might be crucified. It is from this point—when Pilate allowed popular clamor to interfere with his right judgment—that he began that hopelessly downward course of vacillation and bluster, cowardice and cruelty, compromise and subterfuge which have stamped him for all time as a weak and incapable judge, who, in a moment of acute crisis and desperate dilemma, set aside man's crowning gift of free will.

He tried to temporize between what he knew to be right on the one side and felt to be wrong on the other; he decided neither in favor of Christ or Caesar, he washed his hands to escape the difficulty of making an unpopular decision, and threw the burden of responsibility upon the prosecutors. He did not at once veto the injustice of condemning an obviously innocent man and set Him forthwith at liberty, but pronouncing Him innocent, he tortured Him hoping to get the people to be content with thus much punishment.

Obviously, from the Procurator's own lips, he recognized where the path of justice and duty lay, but he chose deliberately to evade it. To him one feels that Dante's words rightly apply '*che fece per viltate il gran rifiuto*', (he refused out of cowardice).

He was *par excellence* [at the level of] the type of those feeble characters whom justice and mercy equally despise, who side

....

208   John 18:38

neither with God, or man, or the devil, but who are so morally invertebrate [spineless] as to be incapable of using their free will when a vital emergency occurs.

The Jews refused Barabbas, and Pilate feebly asked what he should do with their King. They all cried out begging for a Roman death; thus endeavoring to shift the difficulty of putting a malefactor to death at the Passover on to the Romans. St. Matthew 27:19 here mentions the dream of Claudia, which reads very much as if it were an interpolation, for it breaks into the sense of the context, and has been obviously dragged in; verse 20 clearly should follow immediately after verse 18 in order to complete the episode.

Finding that the offer of Barabbas was rejected, and that his question, "Why, what evil has he done?" only seemed to increase the tumult, Pilate called for water and washed his hands in the sight of the angry multitude. This was a Jewish custom, and implied that the Roman Procurator in condemning this righteous man made his own fellow-countrymen responsible for the punishment that should befall him. The Mosaic law directs that the washing of hands shall be accompanied by these words: "Our hands have not shed this blood, neither have our eyes seen it. Forgive, o lord, thy people Israel whom thou hast redeemed, and suffer not innocent blood to remain in the midst of thy people Israel."

I cannot agree with those writers who think that in washing his hands Pilate deliberately meant to insult the Jewish nation by a public travesty of their own religious ceremonial; rather was it that the uproar was so great—loud voices vehemently accusing Jesus and asking that He might be crucified — that the governor could get no hearing, and so conveyed by a sign which all understood, the intelligence which he could not make audible by word of mouth. Once more the Jews relentlessly insisted upon the Prisoner's death, and accepted the responsibility thus thrown upon them in those terrible words: "His blood be on us and on our children."[209]

St. Luke alone gives the remission of Christ to Herod. The chief priests seeing that Pilate persisted in finding "no fault with

---

209   Matthew 27:25

this man" waxed yet more vehement, and again changed the accusation, "He stirred up all the Jews from Galilee unto this place." Now Herod Antipas, the governor of Syria, was, according to his custom, in Jerusalem for the Passover, and the Procurator caught at this fact as an excuse to escape from enforcing the just verdict he had already given. From the *Forum apprehensionis* [power of the conqueror] he would send the Prisoner to the *Forum originis vel domicilii* [power of the original ruler].

Legally, there was no need to hand over a man arrested in Jerusalem for offenses committed mostly in that city to the jurisdiction of the governor of another territorial district; and Herod wisely and rightly declined to interfere, although, out of idle curiosity, he was "exceeding glad to see Jesus," who answered nothing to the Tetrarch's questions. So back once more to the Praetorium the chief priests and scribes brought their prisoner, and once again Pilate acquitted Him; "I, having examined Him, found no fault in Him, no, nor yet Herod.'

He was innocent, the judge had pronounced the *Absolvo*, and He should at once have been released; instead of this, Pilate, by way of temporizing, made an unjust and illegal proposal: "I will chastise Him and release Him."

THE CONDEMNATION

The four Evangelists are not quite in agreement in their statements about the scourging of our Lord. St. Luke does not tell us that it was ever carried into effect.

Matthew and Mark merely state that when "Pilate had scourged Him he delivered Him to be crucified." St. John relates that the scourging took place earlier in the morning, and was consequently independent of the crucifixion. As a rule, flagellation was part of the Roman death punishment, and it would probably be taken by the multitude as an indication on the part of the governor that he intended to deliver up the Prisoner. It was so brutal a punishment that, according to the classic writers, the prisoners sometimes died under it.

This compromise only increased the clamor of priests and people who "were instant with loud voices asking that He might be crucified." Under this renewed pressure, the Roman governor exclaimed: "You take Him and crucify Him for I find no crime in Him." It was a last and futile effort to rid himself of the difficulty of making up his mind to do justice and face the possible revenge of an angry mob, whom he knew well enough already hated him. This half measure was not at all what the multitude desired. The irreligious scruples, which forbade them to pass into the unhallowed court of the Praetorium on the day of the Passover, would be entirely outraged if required by the heathen governor to defile themselves by putting a criminal to death. They had, as a conquered people, been forced into the bitter position of subservience to Rome in matters of life and death, and they intended that Rome's representative should have the entire responsibility of the condemnation and execution of their prisoner.

Is it possible also, that while insisting upon a Roman death, which in those days was never the fate of a Jewish subject, there may have arisen deep down in the minds of the Sanhedrin the uncomfortable question as to the identity of their Prisoner? **The quiet dignity and the grand silence of the Accused must have struck even the most prejudiced of His enemies. His was not the bearing of a criminal, an impostor, or a fanatic;[210] even to a casual observer it must have gone far to prove His claim to a kingdom "not from here," for no one could have passed through those hours of storm and fury, of insult and physical suffering with such calmness, unless absolutely certain of the truth of His claim.** It may be that the thought passed through their minds that if--in future days--history should prove that Jesus of Nazareth, the despised Galilean peasant-teacher, had been--though rejected and persecuted—their Messiah, the guilt of His death should not rest on their nation. They should be able to point to treason against great Caesar as the crime for which He was condemned, and crucifixion by Roman soldiers as the punishment by which He died.

....

210   Similar line of argumentation to C.S. Lewis' "Lord, liar, lunatic" trilemma.

Again Pilate left the palace to appeal to the people, but they only insisted that by Jewish law the Prisoner ought to die because "He made Himself the Son of God", and then Pilate was afraid. The governor's last interview with Christ is full of pathos [emotion]; the cowardice of the judge, and the gentleness, almost pity, of the Accused towards him are in striking contrast—while His final words to the Procurator, "Therefore he that delivered Me to you has the greater sin" are full of tenderness and forgiveness, nay, almost of excuse. Upon which words, Pilate sought to release him. One final shaft remained yet for the Jewish rulers to aim at the Roman governor, and one that they knew well enough would strike home. "If you let this man go you are not Caesar's friend, whosoever makes himself a king speaks against Caesar." This was the climax—and Pilate, sending the Prisoner out into the open court, himself followed, and seating himself upon the *bema* placed on the Lithostrōton or tessellated pavement that formed the open court in front of the palace, exclaimed: "Behold your King!" only to be shouted down with cries of "Away with Him, crucify Him."

"Shall I crucify your King?" asked the governor, to which the chief priests replied:

"We have no king but Caesar."

For the third time, the Jewish nation rejected Jesus of Nazareth as their Messiah, and at the same moment acknowledged the Imperator of Rome—their conqueror—to be their king. How true those words were destined to prove, they doubtless did not foresee; but from that day forth for the next two-thousand years, the Jews have been in the strange and anomalous [odd] position of a race without a leader, a nation without a country, a people under submission to the Caesar in whose land they dwell as strangers and foreigners, and among whose own subjects they are but at the best of times barely tolerated.[211]

Three times had Pilate declared the Prisoner to be not guilty; but now, overwhelmed by the fury of an Eastern mob, the weak and

....

211   Remember, Mary is writing in 1908, 40 years before Israel became an official nation again.

utterly unnerved Roman Procurator was willing to content the people, and, without rescinding his original verdict, delivered the fateful condemnation.

Ibis ad crucem. (You will be crucified.)

Jesus Christ was condemned to death by the Sanhedrin for blasphemy against God. He was arraigned before the Roman Procurator on a charge of sedition and high treason, of which crimes He was proved innocent. He was executed because Pontius Pilate wished to please the Jewish people.

PILATE AS JUDGE

There are many writers who maintain that the proceedings before Pilate were illegal from the point of view of Roman law, and in proof thereof describe the elaborate organization and lengthy formalities of a trial under the Empire.

They contend that legally, Pilate should have proclaimed to the multitude, by the voice of the public crier, a day on which he would consider the charges brought against the Prisoner, summoning also His fellow citizens to come together at the same time. On the day appointed, the judge in the presence of the Prisoner and in open court should have announced the crime alleged against Him, a statement of which should also have been made in writing. The Sanhedrin would have then been required to produce their witnesses and the accused His, when the judge after weighing the evidence would have pronounced judgment in either of the following terms:

1. *Absolvo* (Aquitted),

2. *Condemno* (Condemned), or

3. *Non-liquet* (The matter is still unclear/unresolved),

as the case might be.

These writers emphasize the fact that it was not in Roman towns only that these regulations prevailed, but in the country districts and conquered provinces as well. This is undoubtedly true so far as the Romans were themselves concerned; but Jesus Christ was not a Roman citizen. He was a Jew, and not even a Roman subject save by conquest, so He could not claim a formal Roman trial nor appeal to Caesar. His case—in its differences—can in no way be compared with that of St. Paul before Felix and Festus. True it is that St. Paul was proud to call himself a Hebrew of the Hebrews, and that like Christ he was arrested in Jerusalem; but unlike Christ, he was a Roman freeborn citizen "which privilege carried with it besides private rights:

1. Exemption from degrading punishments, e.g., scourging and crucifixion;

2. Right of appeal to the Emperor after sentence in all cases;

3. Right to be sent to Rome for trial before the Emperor if charged with a capital offence," (Bernard).

St. Paul could and did claim these rights.

A marked feature in the policy of Rome towards her conquered subjects was to judge them as far as possible according to their own laws, and to allow them the use and methods of their national courts; and while she required her foreign delegates to execute justice, she allowed them great latitude in the method of administering it. The Jewish rulers had already tried and passed sentence on Jesus Christ, and they came to Pilate for the endorsement of their verdict and the necessary permission to carry out the death sentence. If they had not evaded his first question 'What accusation do you bring against this Man?' but had at once answered that He had blasphemed God and by their law He ought to die, probably Pilate seeing that it was purely a question of Jewish religion would have said, "Take Him and stone Him." But His accusers first evaded giving an answer, and then refused a direct reply, which determined the Procurator to look into the matter for himself. Here, evidently, was a case in which a man's life hung in the balance, it was obvious that for envy His fellow-countrymen had delivered Him, and Pilate chose to exercise the conqueror's right of *recognitio*.

There were certain important formalities required in a Roman trial which were faithfully carried out by Pilate. He demanded:

1. The public *accusatio.*
   "What accusation do you bring against this man?'"
2. He addressed to the prisoner the *interrogatio.*
   "Are you then a King?"
   "Are you the King of the Jews?"
3. The *excusatio* on the part of the prisoner was allowed.
   "My kingdom is not of this *kosmos.*"
   "Now is my kingdom not from hence."
4. The just verdict— *absolvo* — was three times repeated.
   "I find no crime at all in Him."

The Procurator was in all these respects a strictly correct judge. He failed because, after having examined the Prisoner, considered the evidence and pronounced Him innocent, he had not the courage to abide by his deliberate verdict, but yielding to the pressure of an angry crowd, suggested first a compromise and then, in spite of his knowledge and against his better judgment, condemned an innocent man to death. Pilate had plenary power to deal with what would appear to him to be a case of Jewish religious enthusiasm in such a manner as seemed to be fitting with its requirements, without being tied down to the strict formalities of a Roman law court, and no injustice can be alleged, nor fault found with the method pursued as far as the pronouncement of the verdict.

The trial was at that point actually completed, and all that followed was but a series of vacillations [indecision], compromises, and evasions made in order to avoid carrying the just verdict into effect. Overwhelmed by the blind passion of the multitude, Pilate, without rescinding his verdict of not guilty, consented to the death sentence.

No verdict of guilty or *condemno* was ever passed upon our Lord by the Roman Procurator; His own national tribunal alone judged Him to be worthy of death. Pilate first acquitted Him, and afterwards weakly yielded to the clamor of the Jews.

It may have been that he was utterly unstrung by such an exhibition of insensate fury and unable to pronounce another verdict. Possibly even he would not compromise himself by an unjust condemnation, after pronouncing a just acquittal; or it may be that in this feeble-minded judge there was a faint sense of justice, and perchance a spark of conscience, which prevented him from deliberately giving a judgment which he knew to be absolutely false.

Lecture III: The Crucifixion and the Site of the Holy Tomb

Topics Covered: Christ delivered to the Roman soldiers, Golgotha, Legend of the Place-Name, Route to the Cross, the Crucifixion, History of the Punishment, Method of Crucifixion, and the Tomb. *Christus, Tiberio imperitante, per procuratorem Pontium Pilatum supplicio affectus est.*

(Christ, under the command of Tiberius, was put to death by the procurator Pontius Pilate.)

CHRIST DELIVERED TO THE ROMAN SOLDIERS

The chief priests and scribes with the multitude having gained their end — the condemnation of Jesus Christ to a Roman death — now probably withdrew from the balustrade of the Praetorium, leaving the Prisoner to the tender mercies of the Roman soldiery who forthwith led Him back from the open court into the palace hall, where, calling together the whole band (*speira*) they proceeded to torment their Victim while the cross was being prepared.

St. Matthew (27:27) says the soldiers arrayed Him in a scarlet robe. St. Mark (15:16) and St. John (19:2) call it purple; probably it was the *chlamys*, which was the distinctive mark of a Roman soldier, and was of the color called by Pliny *coccinea*. Then plaiting a crown of thorns they mockingly saluted Him as King of the Jews. Conjecture has been rife as to what plant was taken to make the crown. It is impossible to say for certain. The *juncus marinus*, the *zizyphus spina Christi*, the *calycotome villosa* known in modern Arabic as the *kundaul*, and the *rhamnus punctata* have all been suggested with more or less plausibility, and any of them might well have been used. Perhaps of these four, the last mentioned was the most likely.

St. Luke is silent as to what took place between the passing of the sentence and the procession to Golgotha. St. John (19:2-4) gives the same events as St. Mark, but makes them take place earlier in the morning and Pilate to be cognizant [aware] of them, leaving us at first sight with the impression that there were two similar, yet distinct, episodes. This is most improbable. It is far more likely that St. Matthew and St. Mark writing so much nearer the time should give the correct sequence, and that the writer of the fourth gospel who put together his recollections of our Lord at a much later period may have, while clearly remembering the facts, inverted the sequence.

It cannot have been long after the offering of the morning sacrifice when the procession started from the Praetorium,[212] followed at a distance by a "great multitude of the people, and women who bewailed and lamented Him" with those shrill, odd sounds that from this time have been practiced by the Jews on the occasion of a death, and which none save themselves seem capable of emitting. It may be also that some of the women who followed their revered Master poured forth as they moved along, an extemporized [composed] lament for him, as it was the special office of Jewish women to improvise and chant the death songs for all save kings and warriors. Had it not been for this exception, we should never have had that exquisitely pathetic lament of David for his friend Jonathan.

According to the Synoptists, the soldiers meeting Simon of Cyrene coming into Jerusalem from the country, made him carry the cross after Jesus. St. John does not mention Simon, but says that Christ "went out bearing the cross for Himself."

Here I want to call your attention to one of those misapprehensions of Scripture which has formed a favorite subject for artists, and a popular text for sermons, and which owes its existence to ignorance. It is currently accepted among Christians that in carrying the cross, our Lord carried the whole cross and sank beneath the burden, and that Simon was pressed to relieve him from its weight. This is not so, as the entire cross was not carried by the prisoners; they only carried to the place of execution the

212   Mark 15:25; John 19:14 complicates the question by stating that it was the sixth hour when Pilate said to the Jews, "Behold your King!"

patibulum, or cross bar, which was usually made of some thin wood. The heavy upright made of a strong beam—or even tree trunk—was driven into the ground beforehand. At the same time, we can well believe that the long-drawn-out mental agony which began in Gethsemane, when further combined with the fatigue of standing bound for so many hours, and then increased by the brutal flagellation,[213] had completely exhausted our Lord's physical powers, so that even the light weight of the *patibulum* might have been beyond His strength to carry. To represent Him as carrying the entire cross is a historical and artistic fiction.

GOLGOTHA

The site of the crucifixion is generally spoken of as a mount or hill, for which statement there is not the slightest scientific foundation. **Nowhere in the Gospels — which *alone* furnish contemporaneous records — is Golgotha alluded to in any way that could possibly give rise to the idea that it was on raised ground.** Early Christian art and not topography is probably responsible for the original presentment of an elevated spot, and the mosaic in the Basilica of St. Pudenziana in Rome, which probably dates from about the fourth century, is one of the first representations of the cross being erected upon a little rounded knoll or hillock. From that time onwards, artists have invariably depicted the crucifixion as taking place upon a hill, or at any rate on elevated ground, probably in order to carry out the idea that it could be seen from afar.

There is no mention of Golgotha being raised ground until the fourth century, when it is spoken of as a *monticulus*, or little hill, by the Bordeaux Pilgrim. The expression does not occur again until once in the sixth century,[214] after which we do not come across it until Bernard the Pilgrim visited Palestine in the ninth century, and writes of having seen *Mons Calvariae*. From that date, the expression is frequently used by writers belonging to the Western

....

213   The Roman soldiers stripped the prisoner, tied him to a post in a stooping position, and beat him with a scourge composed of leather thongs with sharp pieces of bone, or bits of lead knotted into the ends. Flagellation usually preceded crucifixion among the Romans. Horace calls it the "horrible flagellum."

214   In *The Breviarus*

Church, and has survived unto this day. The early Greek writers, with the exception of Gregory Nazianzen and Cyril of Jerusalem, never allude to Golgotha as connected with a hill or height, and it must be remembered that both these authors lived after the official finding of the holy places by the Emperor Constantine. Unfortunately, this false idea is likely to be current even amongst the educated classes so long as some good people will continue to write, and other good people will continue to teach their children that "there is a green hill far away,"[215] upon which our Lord was crucified.

This assertion is a fair specimen of one of those many cases that we come across both in history and science where a supposition stated sufficiently often and forcibly, becomes in time an established fact.

Golgotha was not a hill, and if it had been, it would not have been green. It was far more likely to have been a site in one of the ravines or deep ditches which run from north to south of the city, it may even be it was a ridge in the Tyropaean Valley itself; and though most writers place it on the north side of the city, there is no reason why it should not have been on the south side. Such a spot would have allowed both priests and people to watch the crucifixion without being near enough to incur ceremonial defilement. Joseph of Arimathea's garden, in which was his newly excavated tomb, lay close to the spot selected by the soldiers; and like all Jewish graves, it would be rock-hewn in the face of one of the limestone terraces, on which the garden was formed.

The Gospels give us no definite landmarks as to the exact site of Golgotha, and it is easier to say where it could not have been than where it actually was. We know that it was outside the *second* wall of the city, that it was near a main road, and yet "near to the city," and probably for the sake of publicity was close to the gateway. It must have been an open space for people to have been able to see "from afar off," and it was adjoining a garden in which was a new tomb. We know that the lie of the ground was such that the Jews could revile him *saying* (not calling out, or shouting): "You that

---

215   From a hymn by Cecil Frances Alexander in 1848.

destroys the Temple and builds it in three days save Yourself," etc., and that the road-farers could rail on Him; that it was in such a position that the women and the disciple whom He loved could stand near the cross without becoming polluted, and that even in His death agony His words were audible to them.

It must have been immediately outside one of the city gates — possibly on the north side — which could be easily reached from the Praetorium, whether that building at the moment was the Palace of Herod, or the disused palace of the Hasmonaean Princes. One thing would be quite certain, and that is that the soldiers, after the angry scenes of the morning would, for fear of an outbreak of popular fury, put the Prisoner to death as near at hand, and as quietly, as they possibly could. Pilate also would wish to avoid a disturbance among the Jews with Herod in Jerusalem ready to report him to Tiberius should a breach of the peace occur. Also, the Jews with the Passover drawing near must have been anxious to procure the execution of the sentence as speedily as possible, for they well knew that many long hours must elapse before death would release their Victim, and enable them to bury His body before nightfall. Instead, therefore, of looking for an impossible "green hill" outside Jerusalem upon which to locate the crucifixion, we are more likely to be nearer to the true site on the floor of a rock-terrace, forming the side of a ravine close against one of the city gates in the second wall. From both wall and gateway, the priests and people could easily look down upon the scene and deride the Prisoner without being defiled.

> a. The centurion and soldiers led Jesus away to 'a place called Golgotha, that is to say the place of a skull.'[216]
>
> b. 'The place Golgotha, which is being interpreted the place of a skull.'[217]
>
> c. 'The place which is called the Skull.'[218]
>
> d. 'The place called the place of a skull which is called in the Hebrew Golgotha.'[219]

....

216   Matthew 26:33
217   Mark 15:22
218   Luke 23:33
219   John 19:17

The name in Hebrew is *Gulgōleth*, in Aramaic—the current language in Palestine at that day—*Gulgōlta*, the Greek translation of which is *Kranion*, and the Vulgate *Calvaria*. In plain English, it was the Skull Place.

LEGEND OF THE PLACE-NAME[220]

Of the history of this curious place-name, we have neither authentic nor contemporary records. The early Christian writers who have written much and speculated more upon the subject have, in assigning reasons for this name, given play to their lively imaginations mixed up with old traditions. Except in the Gospels, Golgotha is not mentioned by any Christian writer until the time of Origen (A.D. 185-253) who visited Palestine in the early years of the third century. There are no purely *Christian* tradition concerning the name prior to fourth century, and then we have only the very fantastic account given by Eusebius of the official finding of the site, by order of the Emperor Constantine.

That Golgotha received its name because the skulls of criminals, who had suffered capital punishment by decapitation, were allowed to lie about unburied there, is a theory that is not worth the paper and ink with which it has been written. Anyone possessing the slightest acquaintance with either Jewish punishments or customs knows that such a thing would have been impossible.

That the skull-like appearance of the ground originated the name is another much loved and equally fanciful theory, which owes its existence to fourth century writers—mostly Latin, and therefore for the most part unacquainted with Jerusalem. Evidently it must have become fashionable for Epiphanius of Salamis (c. 315-403), a Hebrew, argued against it, declaring it to be untrue: "There is nothing to be seen in the place resembling this name (skull), for it is not situated upon a height that it should be called a skull, answering to the place of the head in the human body, neither has it the shape of a lofty watch tower, for it does not even rise above the places round about it. Indeed, over against it stands

....

220   Much of this section comes from Sir C.W. Wilson's *Golgotha and the Holy Sepulchre.*

the Mount of Olives. . . Lastly, even that hill which once stood on Mount Zion, but at the present day has been cut down, was higher than Golgotha."[221]

We are more likely to get nearer to the real origin of the name by inquiring of the old Jewish writers than of the Christian Fathers, though it is doubtful if they can do more than give local legends as handed down to them from time immemorial.

There is a very ancient tradition, which states that when Adam was banished with Eve from the Garden of Eden, he went and dwelt in the land of Judaea, and that death overtook him in the Mount of Jebus, where he was buried. Now, when Noah was warned of God to prepare the ark and enter into it, he dug up the bones of Adam and took them with him for safe-keeping. After the subsidence of the waters, and before Noah and his sons parted each to go his own way and re-populate the earth, the Patriarch divided the bones among Shem, Ham, and Japheth. To the former he gave the skull, allotting Judaea to him at the same time. When, therefore, Shem arrived in his own country he reburied the skull at Jebus, which after wards became Jerusalem — the sacred city.[222]

Another ancient legend is that, when Adam lay dying he called together his son Seth and his immediate male descendants to the fourth generation, and bade them embalm his body and lay it in the cave El-Kanûz, further requiring of them that whichever of them will be alive when they next migrated was to take his body and re-bury it in the center of the earth from where "shall come my salvation, and the salvation of all my children." Noah took the body into the ark, and when dying, bade Shem and Melchizedek the son of Peleg to take the body secretly and go forth with it, "until the angel of the Lord shall show you the place of burial,

---

221   *Adversus Haereses*, lib. l., tome iii., xlvi. 5.
222   Moses Bar Cepha, Syriac Orthodox Bishop (c. 813-903), in *De Paradiso*, i., cap. 14. Also, Epiphanius of Salamis stated, "Our Lord Jesus Christ was crucified on Golgotha, nowhere else than where Adam's body lay buried. For after leaving Paradise, living opposite it for a long time and growing old, Adam later came and died in this place, I mean Jerusalem, and was buried there, on the site of Golgotha. This was probably the way the place, which means 'Place of a Skull,' got its name, since the contour of the site bears no resemblance to a skull," (*Panarion*, Book I, §45, "Against Severians").

and ye shall know that this spot is the middle of the earth." Which happened on Mount Moriah.

This tradition that Golgotha the skull place, was the grave of Adam's skull was well known to the early Greek fathers.

Origen—a Hebrew scholar—knew it, so also did Athanasius, Epiphanius, Chrysostom, and other fourth and fifth century writers; though it is noticeable that both Eusebius and Cyril of Jerusalem do not mention it, but their position with regard to Constantine would perhaps prevent that. Only a few of the Latin writers seem to have taken it into account; Augustine in the *Sermones Supposititii*, Sermo, vi., alludes to the "ancient tradition that the first man Adam was buried on the very spot where the cross was set up, and the place was therefore called Calvary." Jerome knew of the Hebrew tradition, but scorned it, proposing an interpretation of his own which is wholly untenable.[223]

In the sixth and subsequent centuries, it was evidently a current tradition that Adam was buried in Jerusalem, and that on the site of his grave Jesus Christ was crucified, thereby bringing salvation to Adam's descendants, and thus fulfilling his prophecy. So widely was this legend known that it found its way into the Abyssinian church and appeared in the Ethiopic *Book of Adam*.

The probability is, therefore, that Golgotha received its name from being the *traditional* burial-place of Adam's skull. That it was a well-known place is evident, as neither of the Evangelists — not even St. John who is so exact in his explanations — thought it necessary to mention its locality. Adam legends seem to have found favor with early ecclesiastical writers, and there are, I believe, four separate works upon the traditional history of our first ancestor, besides a *Book of Adam*, referred to in the Talmud. With the exception of this last, they are post-Christian in date, but supposedly based on Jewish tradition.

ROUTE TO THE CROSS

....

223   Migne, *Pat. Lat.* xxv., col. 209.

Speculation has been busy throughout the ages as to the route taken from the Praetorium to Golgotha, and a vast amount of ingenuity based mostly upon ignorance of the topography of Jerusalem has been wasted in describing minutely the Via Dolorosa. It is only necessary to say that the present so-called Via Dolorosa, upon which so much sentimentality has been poured out, cannot possibly have been the street in Jerusalem along which our Lord passed. I am well aware that an old tradition represents Him as having been marched through the main thoroughfares of the holy city, so that the crowds assembling for the Passover might see and take warning by His fate. It is also true that the Romans considered it to be part of the death punishment to escort a criminal through the chief streets in order that he might feel his disgrace more acutely; but Christ was not a Roman, nor had He been found guilty of any crime by the Procurator (who was merely sacrificing Him to please the people) nor was He being put to death on Roman territory. When Pilate delivered Christ to be crucified, he had finished with Him, and it was the executioners, and not the governor, who chose the site and the route.

Seeing the ferment and uproar that the trial of the Prisoner had caused, and the fury with which His death sentence was forced from the Roman governor by His own countrymen, and knowing also that Jerusalem was crowded for the Feast, it was only likely that the centurion would select the nearest available spot outside the city wall for the site of the execution, and get it over as quickly as possible. We do not know for certain which palace served that morning as the Roman judgment-hall, but of this we may be quite sure that the centurion removed our Lord by the nearest and least frequented route in order to prevent either a riot or a rescue; and "modern tradition is clearly at fault in identifying the first part of the Via Dolorosa with a street that lies above the ditch, which at the time of the crucifixion, must have protected the Antonia and the second wall."[224]

THE CRUCIFIXION

At Golgotha, the Skull Place, they crucified Him, having spared him the worst indignity inflicted upon a condemned criminal, that

224   Wilson, Sir C.W., *Golgotha and the Crucifixion*, p. 290.

of stripping Him of His clothes *before* leaving the place of detention. The clothing and in fact anything of which the Prisoner could be despoiled, were the perquisites of the executioners, for which there is a distinct provision made in Roman law,[225] so that there was nothing unusual, nor was there any especial insult intended when the four soldiers did finally part his garments among them at the site of the crucifixion.

The Synoptists are not agreed as to the hour at which the crucifixion took place. St. Matthew does not mention it, but states that there was darkness over all the land from the sixth to the ninth hour, and that at the ninth Jesus yielded up His spirit.[226]

St. Mark says that it was the third hour when they crucified Him, and that darkness prevailed from the sixth to the ninth hour when "He gave up the ghost."[227]

St. Luke, like St. Matthew, gives various details as to what took place after the crucifixion, and before the darkness settled down upon Jerusalem at the sixth hour, but agrees with the Synoptists that it was at the ninth hour when our Lord cried with a strong voice and gave up His spirit.[228]

St. John does not mention either the time of the crucifixion or the hour of death, nor does he allude to the darkness that enveloped the land.[229]

Seeing that St. Matthew and St. Luke both mention such facts as the setting up of the *titulus,* the division of the garments, the reproaches of the robbers, and the derision of the passers-by, scribes, and elders as all taking place after the actual crucifixion and before the sixth hour, probably the third hour given by St. Mark is the correct. Crucifixion was such a lingering death that

----

225   *De bonis damnatorum,* xlvii. 20.
226   Matt. 27:45-50
227   Mark 15:25-33
228   Luke 23:46
229   But he does state that at the sixth hour on the day of preparation Pilate said to the multitude "Behold your King!" which adds yet another difficulty. John 19:14.

three hours, medically speaking, would have hardly sufficed for the victim's release. It was not an uncommon thing for a prisoner to hang on the cross for three or even four days, dying in the end from exhaustion, starvation, and exposure to the elements. Cases have even been recorded of a criminal being taken down as dead, and reviving. Had Christ been a Roman subject, burial would have been denied Him, as the body would have been left on the cross until the birds and beasts had devoured the flesh, and the action of sun and rain had caused the skeleton to fall to pieces.

Most people base their ideas of the crucifixion upon Medieval art, and the mass of devotional literature which has been published upon the subject; these if tested by medical and historical evidence will be found in many points to be inaccurate or only applicable to the aggravated punishment inflicted at a later period. I have not the slightest desire to minimize the physical sufferings of Jesus Christ, and I desire to speak with all reverence of the events of that day, but we have slipped into a conventional way of accepting statements, and it will be well to look at the actual facts rather than at the emotional and artistic presentments of Christ's death. The mental and spiritual agony of the God-man was beyond human power to understand or to measure, so intense that compared with it, His physical sufferings were probably as naught; but the contemplation of exaggerated bodily suffering can only produce a morbid psychic condition, instead of carrying us up on to the higher plane involved in the endeavor to realize the insuperably greater agony of a perfectly pure spirit.

HISTORY OF THE PUNISHMENT

Let us look at the history of this punishment of crucifixion up to the time of the siege of Jerusalem. There is no need to go into the added suffering of it under Titus and the later emperors. Jesus Christ was not crucified under Varus or Diocletian, but in the days of Tiberius and by the method in use in his reign.

The very word in itself is, on the surface, misleading, because in Roman law every man condemned to death was called *cruciarius*, and whether he was merely hanged on an *arbor infelix*[230], or by whatever form of capital punishment he was executed, that death was called the cross — *crux*.[231]

We must go back to the very beginning of history for the origin of the punishment. The Greek word gives it best: *stavros*, a great stake, which in Latin becomes *palus*, from which we derive our words pale, paling, and impale. To impale was to suspend the corpse of a victim to an upright stake or beam, or to drive a stake through it. This punishment came from the East. It was common in Chaldea and Persia, and was not unknown in Egypt.

It was practiced by the Philistines, the Numidians, and the Phoenicians, and from these latter found its way into Greece, where it was at first used as a posthumous form of disgrace. I believe that Alexander the Great was the first to bind — not nail — a living man to the stake.

Crucifixion was in fact the outcome or evolution of impaling. There are ancient Babylonian bas-reliefs representing the king and queen feasting in a beautiful garden surrounded by their courtiers and favorites. In the trees above them are suspended the heads of their enemies, whose bodies were either staked or hung up in a public place as a warning to the passers-by. In Egypt, there may be seen at Edfou and other temples representations of prisoners, with their hands and feet tied behind their backs, bound to a great stake driven into the ground; and the episode of the baker in the history of Joseph is familiar to all. He was to be beheaded and his body afterwards impaled.[232]

The suspension and exposure of a dead body either from a tree or a stake was by no means unknown among the Jews. In fact, Deuteronomy 21:22 expressly provides for this form of punishment, and St. Paul directly applies it to our Lord's crucifixion.[233]

....

230   A tree which neither grows from seed nor bears fruit.
231   Cicero, *Pro Rabirio*, 3, 4; Plautus, *Aulularia*, 3, 5, 46; Apuleius, *Met.* 10 — Terence, *Eunuchus*, 2, 3, 91.
232   Genesis 40:19
233   Galatians 3:13

When "Israel abode in Shittim," and bowed themselves down before the Baal of Peor, Moses was commanded to take the chiefs of the people and "hang them up before the sun," i.e., in broad daylight, that all might see and fear, and he bade the judges saying, "Each of you must put to death those of your people who have yoked themselves to the Baal of Peor."[234] Probably, as in Exodus 32:27, they were first put to the sword and then impaled.

The people of Ai, in the days of Joshua, were put to the sword, and the corpse of their king hanged on a tree until the sunset, when Joshua took it down, cast it just outside the gate of the city (the most public place) and raised a cairn over it.[235]

There is even a better example still in 2 Samuel 21: "When famine had ravaged the land of Canaan for three years, David sought the Lord. And the Lord said, 'It is for Saul and for his bloody house, because he put to death the Gibeonites.'" So David sent for the Gibeonites and inquired of them what atonement he could make for the dead king's act, and they replied that neither silver nor gold could wipe out the deed, and requested that seven of Saul's sons should be handed over to them that, "they might hang them up unto the Lord." So they were put to death in the beginning of the barley harvest, and their bodies "hanged before the Lord"; and Rizpah, the mother of two of the dead men, stationed herself below the stakes until the autumn rains came, in order to prevent the birds of the air and the beasts of the field from touching them. As a reward for this devout attention, David took the bones and had them buried.

The fate that befell Saul and Jonathan his son, at the hands of the Philistines, was the same, their bodies were hung up in the street or broad place of Beth Shan.

The Greeks appear to have borrowed the idea of exposing the dead body of a criminal upon a stake or gibbet from the Phoenicians, and to have, afterwards, added suffering to ignominy [disgrace] by first binding the prisoner alive to the tree or stake. Alexander

....

234   Numbers 25:5
235   Joshua 8, A cairn is a mound of stones built as a memorial or landmark.

the Great is said by Josephus to have thus crucified two thousand conquered Syrians, but the numbers are doubtless exaggerated. From Greece this form of death passed to Rome, where it was developed from the suspension of a criminal upon an *arbor infelix*, i.e., a tree which neither grows from seed nor bears fruit[236] — to the binding of him alive, to an upright stake with a transverse beam along which were stretched the arms — a cross in fact.

At first, the Romans made but sparing use of this form of crucifixion as a death punishment; citizens were exempt from it, and it was reserved for slaves, highwaymen, those condemned for treason, and for criminals of the lowest and most violent type. It was looked upon with intense horror, and Cicero in his celebrated letter to Verres speaks of it as *crudelissimum teterrimumque* (most cruel and terrible). Not only was there great *infamia* (ignominy/ disgrace) connected with this form of execution, but the sufferings of the victim were so protracted (prolonged) — sufferings which he must endure to the bitter end, as consciousness was generally retained until the moment of death. For three, and even four days prisoners have been known to hang bound to the cross, exposed to the heat by day and the cold by night, jeered at and tormented by every passer-by, until finally they died from exhaustion and exposure to the elements.

Under the emperors, crucifixion was placed on the list of the death penalties,[237] and then citizens were not exempted from it, though in order to mitigate (lessen) the ignominy in their case, it was sometimes carried out privately in the prison itself, instead of in some public place. The victim was accursed, and the *infamia* was so great that it was considered an outrage on the privileges of a *Civis Romanus*.[238] When Verres crucified some Roman citizens in Sicily it aroused a perfect storm of fury, and called forth from Cicero the following strong protest: *"Facimus est vinciri civem Romanem; scelus verberari; prope parricidum necari; quid dicam in crucem tolli?*

....

236   Pliny, *Hist. Nat., lib.* xxvi.
237   'Summa supplicia sunt Crux, Crematio, Decollatio.'
238   Roman Citizen

Verbo satis digno tam nefaria res appellari nullo modo potest."[239] [It is a crime to bind a Roman citizen; to scourge him is a wickedness; to put him to death is almost parricide. What shall I say of crucifying him? Such a guilty action cannot by any possibility be adequately expressed by any name bad enough for it.]

THE METHOD OF CRUCIFIXION[240]

In the time of Jesus Christ, crucifixion was of rare occurrence in Palestine, and was practically unknown as a punishment for the Jews, who were allowed to be put to death by their own methods of execution. After the siege of Jerusalem, and during the succeeding years of revolt, the Romans became so exasperated with the Jews that they treated them with great harshness, and frequently crucified them; though the statements of Josephus, our chief authority in this matter, must be received with caution. It is not an unlikely supposition that Jesus Christ was one of the first — if not the very first — Jew to suffer this dreaded death penalty. After the fall of Jerusalem, and under the later emperors, crucifixion as a form of capital punishment was only too frequently resorted to, and often took place under circumstances of great cruelty. Thus later when Tertullian, Justin, Plautus, and others describe some of the horrors of crucifixion, and apply them to Christ, it must be remembered that they are writing of the aggravated (more severe) form of it that obtained in their day, and not of the method in use when Christ was put to death.

Three forms of cross were used by the Romans:

> a. The *simplex* — a long beam or stake to which the victim was firmly bound, his arms being fastened above his head.
>
> b. The *immissa* or *capitata* — the Latin cross with the transverse or *patibulum* fastened at right angles about three-fourths of the way up the *stavros*. This is the form which popular art has chosen for our Lord's cross, though we

239   Cicero, Marcus Tullius. "The Fifth Book of the Second Pleading in the Prosecution against Verres." Ed. Crane, Gregory R. <u>Perseus Digital Library</u>.
240   Also see Lee Strobel's *Case for Christ* for more information on this subject.

have not the very slightest clue as to which kind the soldiers used. Remembering how sparsely wooded Jerusalem and its environs (surrounding areas) are, it was not unlikely to have been the *simplex* as three crosses were required.

c. The *summissa* or commissa, or as it is sometimes called the *Tau* cross, in which the patibulum was morticed (joined) into the point of the upright beam.

d. The *decussata* — better known as St. Andrew's cross, in which the upright and the *patibulum* were merely grooved into or nailed to each other in such a manner as to form two acute angles.

The *stavros* or stake was generally made from oak, or from some strong tough wood which was driven down firmly into the ground, where it remained for future use. It was usually from 7 ½ to 9 feet high, and the victim was so placed as to have his head and shoulders above the crowd. In the days of Galba, the *stavros* was sometimes made much higher in order to add to the degradation of the victim, and in one case mentioned by Suetonius it was whitened so as to attract more attention. For the *patibulum* or cross bar, some common kind of wood usually sufficed; it was formed either from two parallel laths set a few inches apart and closed at the ends, through which the prisoner's head was sometimes passed[241], or less frequently of a simple board. This was carried by the condemned man himself to the place of execution. In some cases, a block or saddle was fixed to the *stavros*, called the *cornus* or *sedilis excessus* which, while relieving the great strain on the heart and internal organs, prolonged the suffering. The feet were placed side by side and bound to the upright. The block or wedge seen beneath them in pictorial and plastic representations of the crucifixion exists in artistic imagination, and not in history.

Medieval and Modern art and the ecclesiastics of the Western Church insist upon the nailing of our Lord's hands and feet to the cross. **The four Gospels give no clue as to the form of the cross nor the method of execution.** Tiberius was the first to invent the barbarous plan of nailing the hands, as he maintained that death

241   Similar to a medieval pillory.

by being merely bound to the cross was no punishment, but simply an escape from it. The lowest of Roman criminals condemned for violence and murder were thus executed. It is more than doubtful whether as early as A.D. 29 or 33 this aggravated form of crucifixion had passed into the provinces, and very unlikely that it would have been inflicted upon a Jew who was condemned to death—not for any crime of violence or treason against imperial Caesar, but merely because the Procurator wished to please the Jewish mob. If any of the victims were nailed, it was more likely to have been the Roman malefactors than Jesus.

The Evangelists give very little help in the matter.

The only direct allusion to this subject is not given by the Synoptists. It is the incident of Thomas recorded in the Fourth Gospel, wherein that disciple declines to believe in the risen Christ, unless he sees for himself the marks of the nails in the hands and the spear in the side.[242] There is no mention of the feet you will notice.

St. Luke records the sudden appearance of the risen Christ in the midst of His eleven disciples, who were frightened, supposing that they beheld a phantom, and to reassure them He bade them see and feel his hands and feet—not as many suppose for His identification by the nail marks—but that they might realize that he was an actual living being, for "a spirit does not have flesh and bones, as you see I have."[243]

"He showed them his hands and his feet," is not to be found in many of the older manuscripts of this Gospel.

It is, of course, within the region of possibility that our Lord's hands were nailed besides being bound to the cross, but the silence of the four Gospels upon the subject, and with only this one late allusion to it, and that made by a writer who had survived the horrors of both Jewish and Christian persecutions and so may well have had the aggravated form of crucifixion in his mind, leaves it an open question. There is no doubt that the feet were not nailed. It is, I

....

242   John 20:25
243   Luke 24:39

believe, an impossibility — even if a nail large enough could on the spur of the moment have been forged — to drive one through both feet at once as depicted in crucifixes and paintings. It is almost as impossible to nail through even one foot, partly on account of its position against the *stavros* and partly on account of the hardness of the bones in the arch of the foot and the heel. It would certainly be absolutely impossible to nail the feet to the *stavros* without the block of wood seen in so many pictures, which block does not appear in contemporary history or classic literature.[244]

Although Tiberius invented the horrible cruelty of nailing the hands to the cross bar, the victim was bound to it first. It would be impossible to fasten a man — with only a nail passed through the palm of each hand — to a cross beam, without disastrous results ensuing. The weight of the body in such a position would fall forward, and would soon tear through the metatarsal tissue of the hands.[245] The aggravated cruelty lay not only in the greatly increased suffering, but also in the fact that so little blood was lost that the victim's death was in no way hastened.

Realistic but thoroughly inaccurate descriptions in some of the hymns and devotional books of the Western Church, speak of the blood that poured or fell from our Lord's wounds; but in reality, in nailing through the hands only a very few drops of blood would exude, and these so slowly that they would coagulate at once in the open air. In the same way, writers have jumped to the conclusion that the spear that pierced the victim's side also pierced the heart. We have absolutely no foundation for such a statement. The only Gospel that mentions this episode[246] gives no details, and the fact that blood and serum issued from the incision is no proof that they came from the heart; they may equally well have come from the

....

244 Even though her point about Jesus' feet not being nailed could still stand, after Mary wrote this, two crucifixion victims were discovered with a nail driven through their heel bone. "In 1968, archaeologist Vassilios Tzaferis excavated some tombs in the northeastern section of Jerusalem... [and] came across the remains of a man who seemed to have been crucified. His name, according to the inscription on the ossuary, was Yehohanan ben Hagkol," (Forbes.com). It was dated to the 1st century A.D. In 2018, another crucified foot was found during a salvage excavation of tomb in Italy.
245 Many modern scholars attempt to answer this conundrum by saying that the nail was not driven through the palm, but between the wrist bones instead.
246 John 19:34

pleura[247] surrounding the lung. Many of the old masters represent in their paintings the wound as on the *right* side [the heart being on the left].

Doubtless that translation of Psalm 22:16, "They pierced My hands and My feet," which has been thought often to have a Messianic meaning, is responsible for the preconceived idea common to most people that our Lord's hands and feet were nailed.

The Masoretic or pointed text reads *ka' ârî* 'like a lion,' which is worse than no help at all, as it does not make sense.

Duhm and many other Hebrew scholars would read here *ka' ârû* instead — a verb which is derived from the root *kûr*, meaning in its first idea *to be round*; therefore handcuffs or cords or anything which binds or *goes round* the feet and hands would be in accordance with the spirit of the word. Many ancient versions give "they bound" instead of "they pierced."

"They fettered My hands and My feet" would be a rendering that will meet with the requirements of the original. The same idea is to be found in Zechariah 12:10. It was an allusion to the old punishment described before: the hanging up of the victim with his hands above his head.

The Jews of the captive period knew nothing of the "hanging up" or crucifixion with nails of a living man. Jeremiah speaks of "binding up" as the fate of princes after the downfall of Jerusalem.[248] Darius the Mede, proclaimed that if any man should alter the decree made by Cyrus in favor of the Jews that a beam should be pulled out from his house, and "let him be lifted up (or hung up) and fastened thereon." Gregory Nazianzen writing in the fourth century, uses the technical expression, "and when they had hung up the Lord," etc.[249]

....

247 "A thin layer of tissue that covers the lungs and lines the interior wall of the chest cavity. It protects and cushions the lungs. This tissue secretes a small amount of fluid that acts as a lubricant, allowing the lungs to move smoothly in the chest cavity while breathing," www.cancer.gov.
248 Lamentations 5:12
249 *Christus Patiens,* l. 657 *et seqq.*

The reading "they bound" of some ancient versions confirms this meaning which Jerome translates as *fixerunt.*

Cobb writes, "Probably *fixerunt* would never have been used but for the idea that our Lord's sufferings were foretold here in detail. It was believed that His hands were pierced: therefore, it was argued His feet were also. But there is no authority for this latter belief in the New Testament, and apart from this verse nowhere else either. To regard God as planning the details of the passion of His Son centuries beforehand, and inspiring men to write them down, is to take a low and unworthy view of His action. It introduces also a psychological miracle which is unthinkable."[250]

Early Christian art in mosaic and fresco was far more reverent and reserved in the presentment of our Lord's crucifixion than were Medieval painters, and are Modern religious writers. At first the old artists used only signs or symbols to represent it, sometimes only the Greek letter *Tau* ; as years went on you will find a simple cross depicted, then later the sacrificial lamb placed in front of or near to a plain Latin cross, until after many developments a realistic age portrayed the Savior clothed in the long robe or *colobium,* which was gradually shortened to the loin cloth or *perizona.* Since then, art encouraged by the Western Church has degraded itself by spending its genius of conception and craftsmanship upon the terrible and ultra-realistic presentments of the crucifixion, which even if they were accurate in detail are horrible to look upon, and should be discouraged as tending towards morbid sentimentality. We ought to be as historical and sober in our religious beliefs as we try to be in our scientific and intellectual ones. We cannot be worse Christians for striving after this, and we might be better.

St. Matthew says that when they came to Golgotha "they gave him wine to drink mingled with gall"; St. Mark calls it "wine mingled with myrrh." St. Luke and St. John make no allusion to it. It is more than probable that the myrrh of St. Mark is identical with the gall of St. Matthew, for the Hebrew root for both words is the same, and means 'bitter.' Two ancient physicians, Galen and

....
250   W.F. Cobb, *The Book of Psalms*, pp. 62-64

Dioscorides, speak of the soothing effects of frankincense and myrrh, both of which are bitter to the taste. Some writers have seen in that verse, "give strong drink to him that is ready to perish," when considered with the words that precede it,[251] an indication of its use among the Jews as an anodyne (to lessen pain) for those condemned to capital punishment, and there is a passage in the Babylonian Talmud which lends to this view.

In the days when crucifixion was less frequent than it afterwards became, the Roman soldiers used to give an aromatic drink to their victims after having bound them to the *patibulum*, and before raising both to the *stavros*, in order to deaden consciousness. It is to this that the Evangelists refer. It consisted of wine mingled with frankincense to which was sometimes added the *lebkônah*, called by the Hebrews *Rosh*, and by the Arabs *Ras*, i.e., 'the head'. It was also known as the "father of sleep," and was made probably from the *papaver somniferum* or opium poppy, which has an acrid taste. It was practically a temporary anesthetic, and brought a blessed dullness of sensation, if not absolute unconsciousness, to the sufferer in the first awful moments of tension.

This drink our Lord refused.

The soldiers then set up over his head the "superscription" or "accusation" dictated by the Roman Procurator. This is known technically as the *titulus*, and was carried either by the condemned man himself, or was borne before him to the place of execution. It was a thin board or slab of wood whitewashed over with gypsum, on which was inscribed in large black letters the "accusation," not necessarily the "crime," for which the prisoner was to pay the death penalty. St. John alone gives the correct term to it. The four Evangelists vary as to its exact wording, no two formulae being exactly similar though the basis of all is the same—The King of the Jews.

His own people had brought Him to the governor to decree the death sentence because by their law He ought to die for making

....
251   Proverbs 31:6

Himself the Son of God, a point of Jewish ecclesiastical law which to Rome mattered nothing.

They shifted their ground when pressed for a direct accusation of definite crime, and tried to bring in treason against Caesar.

Pilate condemned Christ without retracting or modifying his original sentence—"I find no crime in Him," and therefore as he sentenced the Prisoner to be crucified, though it was merely "to please the people," he naturally had, as the law required, to show cause why capital punishment was inflicted. He therefore recorded the accusation brought against the Prisoner by His own countrymen.

The carrying of the *titulus* was to impress upon the condemned Man His shame and degradation, hence arose the saying *bastázein ton stavrón aùtou* [bearing His cross], and is another of those many misapplied texts; for the taking up the cross meant—not the carrying of a literal cross, but the public shame and exposure to insult, which resulted from having to carry the *titulus*.

The Procurator was determined that no passer-by on that day, and no gazer at that sight, should fail to understand why that Prisoner was executed. In Hebrew (probably Aramaic) the current language of the people, in Greek the polite language which at that time was understood by every educated man, and in Latin the tongue of the conquering and executive race, ran the accusation: The King of the Jews. From the point of view of Roman law it was absolutely the only title that Pilate could have placed above the Prisoner's head, and to the Jews it must have been as gall and wormwood [bitter and repulsive]; but no amount of entreaty could produce anything from the governor, except the unrelenting reply, "What I have written, I have written."

The only note of human and physical suffering during those long hours comes to us through the Fourth Gospel, which records that just before the end, when in the last stage of final exhaustion Christ exclaimed, "I thirst," a soldier dipped a bunch of hyssop— which he could easily pull out from the wall close by — in the *posca* or thin, sour wine which formed part of the daily rations of the common soldiers, and putting it on a reed, raised it to His lips. This gave the momentary stimulus which enabled him to cry with a loud voice, *tetelestai* — "It is finished" — the effort of which ruptured the heart. The Jews realizing that the day was passing, and that the sunset was drawing nigh which brought a festival Sabbath — upon which it would have been a defilement of their land to have victims dying of capital punishment, or dead bodies hanging at the very gates of the Holy City — besought Pilate that their legs might be broken. This was nothing unusual if there was any reason for hastening death, and was done with a heavy wooden mallet called a *crurifragium*. Christ being already dead to all appearances "They broke not His legs"; but in order to make certain that it was actual and not apparent death, a soldier ran a spear into His side, which proved beyond doubt that He had truly yielded up His spirit. This episode is only recorded in the Fourth Gospel, but finds no place in the Gospels of the Synoptists, and it is curious that St. Luke, who always notices and records the physical facts connected with our Lord's life, should have omitted this one.

The Jews had now to all appearances gained their desired end, and had stopped, as they thought, the Preacher and His doctrines. While accepting the consequences of His death they had managed to throw off the responsibility of it from their own shoulders on to those of their hated conquerors, by the hands of whose officers — at their own request — the death punishment had been carried out. They had shown no sympathy with the pure life and high ideals of the Master during His ministry, and at the time of His trial He received neither mercy nor justice from their hands. They not only did not manifest the slightest touch of humanity as they gathered near His cross, but they derided Him in His death agony. And the irony of it was that throughout the long spun-out hours of that grim tragedy, the only mark of consideration that He received was not from one of His own chosen band of disciples, nor from one of His brethren, His kinsfolk, or His acquaintance. It was not even one of His own countrymen, but a Roman soldier who, in the moment of supreme agony, offered him the soothing draught of the "father of sleep," of which, "when he had tasted thereof, He would not drink."

THE TOMB

"And after these things Joseph of Arimathea, being a disciple, but secretly, for fear of the Jews, asked of Pilate that he might take away the body of Jesus: and Pilate gave him leave." John 19:38.

"And Joseph took the body and wrapped it in a clean linen cloth, and laid it in his own new tomb, which he had hewn out of a rock." Matt. 27:59-60.

No minute details are given as to the exact site of the tomb of Christ. The Synoptists merely say that it was rock-hewn; St. John alone gives any clue to its situation— "*In* the place (not *on* which it would be had Golgotha been a hill) where He was crucified, there was a garden, and in the garden a new tomb." There Joseph and Nicodemus, who had not dared to openly confess their belief in the Preacher, placed the body for—as I believe— temporary burial only.[252]

The Jews thought so much of interment in the family tomb that probably Joseph [Jesus' stepfather], who was "of the house and lineage of David," or Zacharias the priest, whose wife Elizabeth was of the daughters of Aaron and a kinswoman of Mary, would either of them have had some large place of "gathering unto the fathers," where, after the Sabbath was past, the body could be finally laid to rest with the customary Jewish ceremonial.

Joseph's tomb was probably excavated in the face of the limestone rock, which arose in abrupt step-like terraces from the ravines. This geological formation is found in many parts of the Holy Land, especially in and around Jerusalem; and in the scarp forming the back of these terraces are to be seen to this day tombs of post-exilic period. They consist of an open antechamber, around which runs a stone *mastabah* or bench, and an inner mortuary chamber. **Probably with the need for haste which the approach of the Sabbath necessitated, the body was laid on the bench in the antechamber. Certainly this would be the case were Joseph's**

....

252   John 19:42 gives ground for this opinion.

148

tomb intended to be only a temporary resting place. The fact also that the women could see the body, and how it was laid, points to its being placed on the mastabah, and not put away in the loculus or kôk. The spices would also be for temporary burial only.

Controversy has raged fast and furious round the site of the tomb, and the question as to whether the present Church of the Holy Sepulchre in Jerusalem does or does not cover it has been fought by archaeologists and ecclesiastics with much energy and no little bitterness. Until we know for an absolute certainty the trend [course] of the *second* wall of the city, we can never lay down the law positively upon the subject, or even suggest a definite spot whereon may have been the tomb that contained *for a few hours* the body of the dead Christ.[253]

During the first four centuries no mention is made of the sacred site. Immediately after the Ascension "those that believed" sold their possessions for the benefit of the needy, and had all things in common.[254] Land is especially mentioned as being parted with by its owners; it is, therefore, more than probable that Joseph sold his garden, which would include his tomb. **And this brings us face to face with the question, which is an important one to consider in connection with this subject: Was it likely that any veneration was paid by the Apostles and early Christians to the temporary resting place of their Master's body? The first Christians were essentially Jews in their strict observance of Mosaic regulations; and the Temple, and not the tomb, was until the fall of Jerusalem, their meeting-place for worship and instruction. Any**

....

253   Two things of apologetic interest are worth noting here: Joseph's tomb was probably only seen as a temporary resting place for Jesus until a proper, final one could be found, therefore the body was laid on the bench in the ante-chamber, or front section of Joseph's family tomb. This showed that the disciples assumed Jesus was truly dead, thinking that they would have to find another, more permanent resting place for the body of their Lord. This was no swooning or fainting episode. Second, the fact that the location of Jesus' tomb is unable to be found today shows that, very early on, it ceased to be important to the early believers, and the reason is probably because it really, truly was empty after the Lord resurrected. Tombs that still contain the body of religious leaders all over the world are known and visited by their followers, and the bodies are still in the tomb, just as they were the day they died.

254   Acts 2:44-45; 4:32-34

reverence of the empty grave would be a practical negation of that very doctrine of the Resurrection, of which the Christ was the exponent and example, and to which they were to be the witnesses to all the world.

The cultus of the tombs of relations and friends, which has become so popular now adays, is but a relic of Paganism that has survived in spite of Christianity, and is only conceivable when graves contain all that has resisted the dissolution of the bodies of the departed; but for Christians to make an *empty* tomb an object of veneration is so absolutely wanting in logic and commonsense that it is inconceivable that the Apostles and their converts should have wasted their time, and compromised their faith in the Resurrection by so doing. They were too full of a burning zeal to go and proclaim the risen Christ, and their definite orders were to disperse after the descent of the Paraclete[255], and to go into all the world making disciples and baptizing into the Triune Name. So persuaded also were they that their Lord would return visibly before many years had elapsed, that their one desire was to lose no time in carrying the gospel of the kingdom north and south, east and west, entreating all men to accept it.

We hear no word from them, nor suggestion even, that their converts should pray or meditate at the tomb—nay, rather, practical missionary activity in spreading the new faith was the distinguishing mark of those early proselytes. Christ's visible departure, which was accompanied by the promise of His invisible presence among them unto the end of the ages, had filled the Apostles with joy, "and they were continually in the Temple praising and blessing God," not praying beside or contemplating an empty grave.[256]

Their whole attitude was so completely that of men who lived with *present* realities, who implicitly believed in a *living* and *ever-present* Master, and fully expected His speedy appearance. To them the temporary tomb must have been nothing, the risen, returning Christ everything, and this belief which was

....

255   The coming of the Holy Spirit at Pentecost
256   Acts 2-4

the driving-wheel of their missionary zeal, coupled with their banishment from Jerusalem and the complete destruction of their city, would effectually prevent any cultus of the tomb, and therefore even the knowledge of its site from being preserved.

To the first *Jewish* Christians, the Temple with its worship and the Mosaic observances and ceremonial were religious essentials, as the early chapters of the Acts of the Apostles show. To the Gentile Christians who had never known or seen the Lord, the veneration of His empty tomb would be a contradiction of the definite teaching of their own special apostle — St. Paul — whose whole force was expended in endeavoring to raise the thoughts and ideas of his converts to a plane above the earth to the worship of a risen, ascended, and yet, spiritually, ever-present Christ, rather than persuading them into the mere intellectual belief in a physical, earthly, and historic Jesus.[257]

The flight of the Christian community to Pella in A.D. 67 or 68 would further lessen any tendency — if one had one arisen — to make the tomb an object of veneration (worship). The siege and capture of Jerusalem and its total destruction by Titus followed by its occupation by the Legion Fretensis and their barracks would certainly alter the ground, and sweep away many Jewish landmarks and sites. It is computed that the Tenth Legion with the auxiliaries quartered in and round Jerusalem cannot have numbered less than seven-thousand men, while the civil population has been estimated at three-thousand. Notwithstanding that Vespasian considered "the province of Judaea" as the private possession of the Emperors, to whose privy purse the revenues belonged. The Holy City lay desolate and in ruined heaps, overgrown with weeds and merely a Roman camp until A.D.136. Hadrian then — "after passing the plough over the ground of the capital"[258] rebuilt it, but not the Temple. To the new city he gave "his own name and the use of the imperial title, for, as he was named Aelius Hadrianus, he named the city Aelia."

It is most unlikely that during all those troublous years a continuous

....

257   Harnack, *History of Dogma*, pp. 82 *et. seqq.*
258   Jerusalem Talmud, *Taanith,* iv.

tradition of the tomb would have been kept up. We do not know when the Christians returned from Pella—in fact we have only the authority of one author, Epiphanius, for asserting that they did so. By the Romans they were at first regarded as a Jewish sect, and no distinction was drawn by the governors between Jews and Christians. It was not until the revolt under Bar Cocheba in A.D. 132, who claimed to be the Messiah, that there was a definite and final rupture between the Jew and the Christian; then, each went his own widely divergent way forever, upon acknowledged and distinct religious lines.

Where Jehovah's house had once stood, arose a Temple to Jupiter Capitolinus, and Jerusalem with its seven districts, from which every Jew was rigidly excluded, became a Roman military colony. Christians were then allowed to come and reside outside the walls of Aelia proper, but by this time knowledge of the site of the tomb must have become hazy and traditional, even if the first Christians had kept it in remembrance.

Neither Golgotha nor the Holy Tomb is mentioned by any of the early pilgrims to Jerusalem, which looks as if their sites did not possess a special attraction for the devout. Eusebius in his *Ecclesiastical History* does not mention them, and in the *Demonstratio Evangelica* he speaks of the Mount of Olives and not the Tomb as being the place where "the Christians flock together to hear the story of Jerusalem," and to worship; for there on the top "our Lord and Savior who was Himself the Word—communicated the mysteries of the Christian covenant, and from there He ascended into heaven."

If the Christians had set any religious value upon the ground of Golgotha and the Tomb, we may be perfectly certain that they would have found some means to preserve among themselves the knowledge of those sites, even if the latter had been sold, and mention would surely have been made of them by early pilgrims. As it is, we have to wait until the fourth century before any desire is manifested to reverence them, and then it is admitted by Eusebius that they were lost. Moreover, the desire to bring them to light did not come spontaneously, either from the little Christian community settled outside Aelia or from the devotion of pilgrims who had travelled to Jerusalem, but merely by the fiat of Imperial Rome.

History is silent as to the real motive which induced Constantine to write to Bishop Macarius of Aelia, and desire him to find the true cross and the holy places; though Eusebius puts it down to "the inspiration of the Savior." One thing is quite certain, and that is there is not a single testimony to the finding of them given by an eyewitness. Every statement made is based either upon divine inspiration or hearsay, and the accounts given of their discovery are so mixed up with the marvelous—not to say miraculous--as to discount credibility.

In the year A.D. 312, Constantine the Emperor of Rome, after having murdered his wife Fausta in her bath and poisoned his son Crispus, became a convert to Christianity.

It may have been to show his zeal for the new faith, or perhaps as an act of atonement for the murder of his relatives, that he commanded "a house of prayer to be erected to God at Jerusalem near the place called the skull." In order the better to accomplish this, Helena his mother, "being divinely directed by dreams" set forth to find the tomb of Christ, "and after much difficulty by God's help recovered it."[259]

Alexander Monachus says that Constantine "sent his mother, a woman in all respects most worthy of praise, with letters and a great sum of money, to Macarius, Bishop of Aelia. In order that they might together search for the Holy Cross and adorn the holy places with buildings." These sites were unknown, and the Bishop of Aelia was commanded by Constantine to "use all diligence in searching for the life-giving Cross, the Lord's tomb, and all the holy places." Was it likely that when Imperial Caesar commanded that certain unknown sites should be laid bare, and sent his mother with a large sum of money for that purpose, that they would remain "lost" for long? The story of the discovery, both of the cross and the sites, may be read at length in the *Theophania* of Eusebius,

....

259   Sozomen, *Hist. Eccles.*, vol. ii.

of which the original Greek text is lost and only the Syriac copy is in existence. Also in his *Life of Constantine*, a most exaggerated panegyric (accolade) of the erstwhile (former) murderer. Sozomen, Socrates, Theodoret, Sulpicius Severus, and Rufinus in their Ecclesiastical Histories, and also Alexander Monachus in his *De Inventione sanctoe Cruris* relate the miraculous finding of the sacred relics. However, their writings are not contemporaneous with the event, and their statements are so mixed up with the legendary and incredible that from a historical standpoint they are not of great value. Even those of Eusebius were not penned until Constantine had officially announced his "marvelous discovery," and their authority was only such information as Constantine, Helena, and Macarius chose to give. The Bishop of Aelia to whom "the place was miraculously revealed," and who was present at the finding of the so-called "true cross," and who must have seen the miracle of the healing of a noble lady by touching its wood (Theodoret), and the raising of a dead body by being placed in contact with it (S. Severus), discreetly never records his experiences.

Eusebius, who lived nearest to the time of Constantine, says that ungodly men — or rather the whole race of demons by their means — and impious (unfaithful) persons determined to hide the sacred cave by bringing earth from the outside and covering it up, that their machinations continued for a long time, and that "none of the governors, praetors, or emperors was found capable of abolishing these daring impieties, save only that one (Constantine) who is dear to God." The hidden cave "was covered with a dreadful thing, a veritable tomb of souls, a building to the impure demon Aphrodite, to whom an image was set up." One asks the question: upon whose authority does Eusebius make this statement? If such a deliberate desecration had taken place, it would never have been allowed to pass unnoticed by previous Christian writers, and yet not one has alluded to either Golgotha or the tomb, let alone their desecration.

Again, who were these "impious persons" who at some unspecified date had of set purpose desecrated the sacred spot? They cannot have been the Roman governors of Aelia nor either of the emperors, for no writer — and certainly not one engaged in praising the reigning Caesar—would have dared to make such a statement. It would have savored too much of *crimen laesae majestatis* with its consequent death penalty. Nor was it likely to have been the Jews, as after the defeat of Bar Cocheba, Jerusalem was ploughed up and the ruins of the Temple finally destroyed.[260] They were then informed that if they so much as came to the city, much more if they entered it, they should be starved to death; and when in the reign of Constantine they were once more allowed to return, they would not have erected a temple in honor of a deity of their conquerors. Knowing how irresistible and relentless the hand of Rome was, it seems impossible to believe that "neither governors, praetors, nor emperors" could abolish these impieties if they wished to do so. We never hear of the subject until Constantine, with his materialistic Roman intellect, wished to establish first a cultus (worship) of the cross, and then of the sacred sites.

Several pilgrimages to Jerusalem are recorded as having been made before Constantine's reign by Christians of the Eastern Church. Melito of Sardis visited it in the end of the second century, Alexander of Cappadocia afterwards Bishop of Jerusalem, and Firmilian in the third, and many others are mentioned in the fourth; but they went "to see where the Gospel history was acted out," "in consequence of a vow," "for the sake of information," "to investigate the footsteps of Jesus," and "to worship on the Mount of Olives." [Unlike modern Christians], evidently Golgotha and the tomb had no attraction for them.

The required sites having been miraculously pointed out to the Bishop of Aelia, and the layers of earth removed, "contrary to all expectation the venerable monument of our Savior's resurrection became visible." The *miraculous* indication of a rock-tomb (as rock-tombs are common enough in Jerusalem) will hardly be deemed by archaeologists sufficient proof that this particular grave selected by Macarius, and over which Constantine built the famous basilica, was in fact the Holy Tomb. We are told that in this same place Helena discovered three crosses and the tablet of Pilate,[261] and she being distressed, and fearing that through ignorance she

....

260 Maimonides, *Bib. Rabbinica*, iii. 67.
261 Socrates, *Hist. Eccles.*, i. 17.

might venerate one of the robbers' crosses instead of the Savior's, confided her difficulty to Macarius, who to relieve her sought a sign from heaven, and shortly obtained it. There was a lady of rank living in Jerusalem at the time, who was ill with an incurable disease, so the Bishop and the Emperor's mother proceeded to her bedside and applied pieces of each cross to her body. When the wood of the Savior's cross touched her, she forthwith arose healed.[262]

Sulpicius Severus gives another version equally incredible. When Helena was in her worst difficulty, "just as if by the appointment of God," the funeral of a dead man was being conducted with the usual ceremonies; all rushing up took the body from the bier. It was applied in vain to the first two crosses, but when it touched that of Christ, wonderful to tell, while all stood trembling, the dead body was shaken off and stood up in the midst of those looking at it. The true cross was thus identified and consecrated with all ceremony.[263]

Unfortunately, neither of these stories carries with it either probability or possibility. However, Helena and Macarius were quite satisfied as to the genuineness of this "venerable and hallowed monument of our Savior's Resurrection," as well as of the "venerable wood of our Lord's Cross," for Constantine wrote to the Bishop and ordered "that a house of prayer should be erected round the cave of salvation, on a scale of rich and imperial costliness." This looks as if the Emperor's original intention had been to include the whole ground of Golgotha and the tomb within one magnificent basilica, which plan was evidently abandoned, as two churches arose, those of the Martyrion and the Anastasis which were connected by a court. They are spoken of by Eusebius as "a temple" raised by the Emperor, in order to be a conspicuous monument of the Savior's Resurrection.[264] The Church of the Anastasis—otherwise known as the Church of the Holy Tomb—was completed about A.D. 335, and was then officially announced to the Christian world as covering the long-lost and newly-found

---

262 Sozomen, *Hist. Eccles.*, ii. 1.
263 S. Severus, *Hist. Sacra.*, ii. 31.
264 Eusebius, *Life of Constantine*, iii. 40.

site of the Savior's tomb.

It is a significant fact that for the first three hundred years after the crucifixion, no interest appears to have been taken in the supposed sites of Golgotha or the tomb, and they were even lost sight of.

In A.D. 335, Constantine established a cultus of them after their miraculous discovery.

Before another four hundred years were past, doubts had already begun to arise in the minds of many of the Palestine pilgrims as to their authenticity, added to the fact that they were inside the city. These doubts seem first to have been voiced by Willibald, who about A.D. 750, writes that "Calvary was formerly outside Jerusalem, but Helena, when she found the cross, arranged that place so as to be within the city."[265]

From that time onwards. we find the question being raised at intervals until 1738, when a bookseller of Altona, Korte by name, went to Palestine to study the sacred places, and as the result of his journey wrote a book entirely rejecting Constantine's sites.[266] Since then, their authenticity has been questioned with both vigor and scholarship, while at the same time numerous places have been suggested all more or less unlikely.

The most widely known and popular theory is that of Otto Thenius and his followers, who would like to identify the so-called Skull Hill and the quarry below it—commonly known as El-Edhemîyeh or "Jeremiah's Grotto" — with Golgotha and the tomb. Unfortunately, General Gordon, who was no archaeologist, was immensely taken with it and vigorously advocated it, but from a purely mystical and fanciful point of view, which cannot for one moment carry any weight. There is not a shred of evidence either direct or indirect, to favor the idea that one of the meanest tombs in the cemetery outside Jerusalem, excavated in an old disused stone

---

265   *Palestine Pilgrims' Texts*, iii.
266   Korte, *Reise nach den Weiland gelobte Lande.* [Journey to the Weiland Promised Lands].

quarry, and possessing unmistakable Christian details, can ever have been the "garden tomb" of the wealthy (Jewish) councilor, Joseph of Arimathaea.

Although we are not justified in positively asserting that the church of the Holy Tomb, the Garden Tomb, and the various other suggested places are *not* any of them the sacred tomb, yet there are strong archaeological and historical reasons for thinking that they cannot be the authentic sites. My own belief is that the knowledge of the sacred places has been lost, and will remain so forever.

F I N I S.

FOLLOW
@SarahREnterline

**sarahrenterline.com
noapologiesbook.com
enterlinepress.com**

FOR UPDATES AND NEWS ABOUT
UPCOMING BOOKS AND SPEAKING EVENTS